Luther's
Christmas Sermons

Martin Luther

Bibliographic Information

Luther's Christmas Sermons was previously published in 1908 by 𝕿𝖍𝖊 𝕷𝖚𝖙𝖍𝖊𝖗 𝕻𝖗𝖊𝖘𝖘 in Minneapolis, Minnesota, translated by John Nicholas Linker. Spelling, grammar, and punctuation from the 1908 edition have been retained, with the exception of antiquated references to Catholics and Roman Catholicism.

an Ichthus Publications edition

Copyright © 2014 Ichthus Publications
ISBN 10: 1505630428
ISBN 13: 978-1505630428

www.ichthuspublications.com

Dedication

To the Memory of "The Luther Readers" in the days of Luther and Spener in Germany, of Rosenius in Sweden, of Hauge in Norway, of Grundtvig in Denmark, of Calvin in France, of Bunyan and the Wesleys in England, and of their spiritual children in all lands, this volume of Christmas Epistle sermons of the English Luther is gratefully and prayerfully dedicated.

Contents

Foreword **9**

1 First Sunday in Advent: *An Exhortation to Good Works, The Day of Grace,* and *Put on Christ, the Armor of Light* † Romans 13:11-14 **13**

2 Second Sunday in Advent: *Exhortation to Bear with the Weak, The Word of Hope,* and *Missions to the Heathen* † Romans 15:4-13 **32**

3 Third Sunday in Advent: *Stewards of God's Mysteries, Faithfulness in Stewards,* and *Man's Judgment and God's* † 1 Corinthians 4:1-5 **66**

4 Fourth Sunday in Advent: *A Christian's Conduct toward God and Man, Prayer,* and *The Peace of God* † Philippians 4:4-7 **94**

5 First Christmas Sermon: *The Appearing of the Grace of God, Ungodliness, Worldly Lusts,* and *The Christian Life* † Titus 2:11-15 **113**

6 Second Christmas Sermon: *God's Grace Received and Good Works to Our Neighbor* † Titus 3:4-8 **140**

7 Third Christmas Sermon: *The Divinity of Christ* † Hebrews 1:1-12 **163**

Foreword

IT IS NOW A YEAR SINCE The Luther Press issued its last volume, "Luther on Christian Education," containing his best catechetical writings. We are happy in assuring the growing list of advance subscribers, however, that the enterprise has received no backset. On the contrary, it has grown in every respect, especially in the efficiency of our co-laborers and in the favor it has received from our institutions of learning. The problem of the young people is the burning question at present; and as Catechetics is about the only branch of theology teaching future pastors their duties to the young, the last volume met a long-felt want, both as a text-book and as a help for side reading on many subjects. For example, the president of one institution ordered one hundred copies and turned his whole school into a Luther-class for one period every Thursday afternoon to study it. The experiment was a success. It is better to study the classics Luther wrote than what others have written about him. "He is, in the best sense, modern, up-to-date, the prophet of our times." Read him, and judge for yourself.

State schools also support chapel services, a Y. M. C. A., and occasional Christian sermons and lectures. But church schools are expected to do more. It is indeed a sad sight to see a foundation going to ruin because the building is not erected. Supporters of Christian schools are now beginning to realize that the only reason for their existence is that they are Christian. No church lays a better foundation in the hearts of the young for Christian culture than the Lutheran and no worse advertisement of a Lutheran school is conceivable than for its students to return home without any growth or development in harmony with their catechism foundation. It has been overlooked that Luther furnishes the best material for the building as well as for the foundation. He is the great evangelist in the evangelization of the Gentiles.

This volume of practical sermons on the epistle texts furnishes the best material for the building, because it exhorts to practice the Christian lessons taught by parent and pastor. In teaching Luther's catechism the aim should be to prepare and interest the pupil to read also his best sermons and commentaries on the Word of God, for God's Word is the chief glory and hope of all Protestants. This was the natural, continued development of our German and Scandinavian parents, whose stable Christian characters their children admire so much, but fail to learn the simple way to imitate. Alas, how many never read a book written by Luther except his Small Catechism!

The connection between this volume of "Christmas Sermons" and the last volume on "Christian Education" is very intimate. It will, we believe, bring Christmas joy to the widening circle of "Luther Readers." In its opening paragraph Luther says:

> "Paul, in Romans 12:7-8, devotes the office of the ministry to two things, doctrine and exhortation. The doctrinal part consists in preaching truths not generally known; in instructing and enlightening the people. Exhortation is inciting and urging to duties already well understood."

By example as well as precept Luther did both. He repeatedly warns against neglecting either. Christian knowledge and zeal, teaching and exhorting, go together and develop a balanced Christianity. Recently at a large young people's convention one asked, "What would be the state of things if all Lutherans lived the simple lessons of the five parts of their catechism?" The answer came, "They would be in paradise." The "Epistle Postil" contains sermons of exhortation and admonition, and are timely both for the individual life and for the work of the Church in evangelization at home and abroad.

Pastors who preach in two languages generally use English in the evening and as they preach on the Gospel texts in the morning these epistle sermons will be especially helpful in the evening services to all pastors who strive not for new truths, but to put old, familiar truths in the plainest and strongest English. Luther wrote these sermons as models for the preachers of his day, models they are now, and models they ought to be until God raises up a greater preacher. They will aid in making English Lutheran preaching and teaching easy for pastors overburdened not only by large pastorates, but by two languages in their large fields.

It is a cherished hope that these practical spiritual writings, teaching true faith in God and right love to our neighbor, may, like "Lutherans In All Lands," contribute to the literature of inner missions. Men like Spener, Wichern, Fliedner and Von Bodelschwingh, developed inner missions on the foundation laid by Luther's writings in the hearts of the German people. The last branch or division of inner missions is literature. This, like all Lutheran literature, must be based on the Luther literature.

For the history of the writing of these sermons the reader is referred to volumes 10, 11, 12 and 13 of the Gospel sermons of the English Luther.

The German text will be readily found in the 12th volume of the Walch and the St. Louis Walch editions, and in the 7th volume of the Erlangen edition.

Due acknowledgement is hereby made of aid received from the translation of Pastor Ambrose Henkel and published in 1869 at New Market, Virginia.

With profound gratitude to the God of all grace for his rich blessings upon this undertaking since its beginning and with the prayer that the same may continue and finally crown the work in every way with success, this volume is now sent forth on its mission of service for the glory of the triune God and the uplifting of fallen man.

J. N. LENKER

Lutheran Home for Young Women,
    Minneapolis, Minn., November 28, 1908

1
First Sunday In Advent

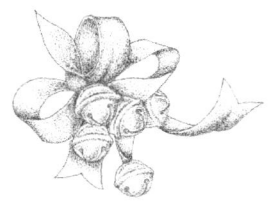

"And this, knowing the season, that already it is time for you to awake out of sleep: for now is salvation nearer to us than when we first believed. The night is far spent, and the day is at hand: let us therefore cast off the works of darkness, and let us put on the armor of light. Let us walk becomingly, as in the day; not in reveling and drunkenness, not in chambering and wantonness, not in strife and jealousy. But put ye on the Lord Jesus Christ, and make not provision for the flesh, to fulfil the lusts thereof" (Romans 13:11-14).

AN EXHORTATION TO GOOD WORKS

THIS EPISTLE LESSON treats not of faith, but of its fruits, or works. It teaches how a Christian should conduct himself outwardly in his relations to other men upon earth. But how we should walk in the spirit before God, comes under the head of faith. Of faith Paul treats comprehensively and in apostolic manner in the chapters preceding this text. A close consideration of our passage shows it to be not didactic; rather it is meant to incite, to exhort, urge and arouse souls already aware of their duty. Paul in Romans 12:7-8 devotes the office of the ministry to two things, doctrine and exhortation. The doctrinal part consists in preaching truths not generally known; in instructing and enlightening the people. Exhortation is inciting and urging to duties already well understood. Necessarily both obligations claim the attention of the minister, and hence Paul takes up both.

For the sake of effect and emphasis the apostle in his admonition employs pleasing figures and makes an eloquent appeal. He introduces certain words—"Armor," "work," "sleep," "awake," "darkness," "light," "day," "night"—which are purely figurative, intended to convey other than a literal and native meaning. He has no reference here to the things they ordinarily stand for. The words are employed as similes, to help us grasp the spiritual thought. The meaning is: Since for sake of temporal gain men rise from sleep, put aside the things of darkness and take up the day's work when night has given place to morning, how much greater the necessity for us to awake from our spiritual sleep, to cast off the things of darkness and enter upon the works of light, since our night has passed and our day breaks.

"Sleep" here stands for the works of wickedness and unbelief. For sleep is properly incident to the night time; and then, too, the explanation is given in the added words: "Let us cast off the works of darkness." Similarly in the thought of awakening and rising are suggested the works of faith and piety. Rising from sleep is naturally an event of the morning. Relative to the same conception are Paul's words in 1 Thessalonians 5:4-10,

> "But ye, brethren, are not in darkness . . . ye are all sons of light, and sons of the day: we are not of the night, nor of darkness; so then let us not sleep, as do the rest, but let us watch and be sober. For they that sleep sleep in the night; and they that are drunken are drunken in the night. But let us, since we are of the day, be sober, putting on the breastplate of faith and love; and for a helmet, the hope of salvation. For God appointed us not unto wrath, but unto the obtaining of salvation through our Lord Jesus Christ, who died for us, that, whether we wake or sleep, we should live together with him."

Paul, of course, is here not enjoining against physical sleep. His contrasting figures of sleep and wakefulness are used as illustrations of spiritual lethargy and activity—the godly and the ungodly life. In short, his conception here of rising out of sleep is the same as that expressed in his declaration (Titus 2:11-13),

> "For the grace of God hath appeared, bringing salvation to all men, instructing us, to the intent that, denying ungodliness and worldly lusts, we should live soberly and righteously and godly in this present world; looking for the blessed hope and appearing of the glory of the great God and our Saviour Jesus Christ."

That which in the passage just quoted is called "denying ungodliness and worldly lusts," is here in our text described as a rising from sleep; and the "sober, righteous, godly life" is the waking and the putting on the armor of light; while the appearing of grace is the day and the light, as we shall hear.

Now, note the analogy between natural and spiritual sleep. The sleeper sees nothing about him; he is not sensitive to any of earth's realities. In the midst of them he lies as one dead, useless; as without power or purpose. Though having life in himself he is practically dead to all outside. Moreover, his mind is occupied, not with realities, but with dreams, wherein he beholds mere images, vain forms, of the real; and he is foolish enough to think them true. But when he wakes, these illusions or dreams vanish. Then he begins to occupy himself with realities; phantoms are discarded.

So it is in the spiritual life. The ungodly individual sleeps. He is in a sense dead in the sight of God. He does not recognize—is not sensitive to—the real spiritual blessings extended him through the Gospel; he regards them as valueless. For these blessings are only to be recognized by the believing heart; they are concealed from the natural man. The ungodly individual is occupied with temporal, transitory things, such as luxury and honor, which are to eternal life and joy as dream images are to flesh-and-blood creatures.

When the unbeliever awakes to faith, the transitory things of earth will pass from his contemplation, and their futility will appear. In relation to this subject Psalm 76:5, reads, "The stout-hearted are made a spoil, they have slept their sleep; and none of the men of might have found their hands." And Psalm 73:20, "As a dream when one awaketh, so, O Lord, when thou awakest, thou wilt despise their image." Also Isaiah 29:8,

> "And it shall be as when a hungry man dreameth, and, behold, he eateth; but he awaketh, and his soul is empty: or as when a thirsty man dreameth, and, behold, he drinketh; but he awaketh, and, behold, he is faint, and his soul hath appetite: so shall the multitude of all the nations be, that fight against mount Zion."

But is it not showing altogether too much contempt for worldly power, wealth, pleasure and honor to compare them to dreams—to dream images? Who has courage to declare kings and princes, wealth, pleasure and power but creations of a dream, in the face of the mad rage of earth after such things? The reason for such conduct is failure to rise from sleep" and by faith behold the light.

"For now is salvation nearer to us than when we first believed."

What do these words imply? Did we believe before, or have we now ceased to believe? Right here we must know that, as Paul in Romans 1:2-3 says, God through his prophets promised in the holy Scriptures the Gospel of his Son Jesus Christ our Lord, through whom all the world was to be saved. The word to Abraham reads, "In thy seed shall all the nations of the earth be blessed" (Gen. 22:18). The blessing here promised to the patriarch, in his seed, is simply that grace and salvation in Christ which the Gospel presents to the whole world, as Paul declares in the fourth chapter of Romans and the fourth of Galatians. For Christ is the seed of Abraham, his own flesh and blood, and in Christ all believing inquirers will be blessed.

This promise to the patriarch was later more minutely set forth and more widely circulated by the prophets. All of them wrote of the advent of Christ, and his grace and Gospel, as Peter in Acts 3:18-24 says: The divine promise was believed by the saints prior to the birth of Christ; thus, through the coming Messiah they were preserved and saved by faith. Christ himself (Luke 16:22) pictures the promise under the figure of Abraham's bosom, into which all saints from the time of Abraham to Christ's time, were gathered. Thus is explained Paul's declaration, "Now is salvation nearer to us than when we first believed." He means practically:

> "The promise of God to Abraham is not a thing for future fulfilment; it is already fulfilled. Christ is come. The Gospel has been revealed and the blessing distributed throughout the world. All that we waited for in the promise, believing, is here."

The sentence has reference to the spiritual day Paul later speaks of—the rising light of the Gospel; as we shall hear.

But faith is not abolished in the fulfilment of the promise; rather it is established. As they of former time believed in the future fulfilment, we believe now in the completed fulfilment. Faith, in the two instances, is essentially the same, but one belief succeeds the other as fulfilment succeeds promise. For in both cases faith is based on the seed of Abraham; that is, on Christ. In one instance it precedes his advent and in the other follows. He who would now, like the Jews, believe in a Christ yet to come, as if the promise were still unfulfilled, would be condemned. For he would make God a liar in holding that his word is unredeemed, contrary to fact. Were the promise not fulfilled, our salvation would still be far off; we would have to wait its future accomplishment.

Having in mind faith under these two conditions, Paul asserts in Romans 1:17, "In the Gospel is revealed a righteousness of God from faith unto faith." What is meant by the phrase "from faith unto faith"? Simply that we must now believe not only in the promise but in its past fulfilment. For though the faith of the fathers is one with our faith, they trusting in a Christ to come and we in a Christ revealed, yet the Gospel leads from the former faith to the latter. It is now necessary to believe not only the promise, but also its fulfilment. Abraham and the ancients were not called upon to believe in accomplished fulfilment, though they had the same Christ with us. There is one faith, one spirit, one Christ, one community of saints; but they preceded, while we come after, Christ.

Thus we—the fathers and ourselves—have had and Still have a common faith in the one Christ, but under different conditions. Because of this common faith in the Messiah, we speak of their act of faith as our own, notwithstanding we were not alive in their day. And similarly, when they make mention of hearing, seeing and believing Christ, the reference is to ourselves, in whose day they live not. David says (Ps. 8:3), "When I consider thy heavens, the work of thy fingers," that is, the apostles. Yet David did not live to see their day. And (Ps. 9:2), "I will be glad and exult in thee; I will sing praise to thy name, O Thou Most High." And there are many similar passages where one individual speaks in the person of another in consequence of a common faith whereby believers unite in Christ as one body.

Paul's statement "Now is salvation nearer to us than when we first believed" cannot be understood to refer to nearness of possession. For the fathers had the same faith and the same Christ with us, and Christ was equally near to them. Hebrews 13:8 says, "Jesus Christ is the same yesterday and today, yea and for ever." That is, Christ exists from the beginning of the world to all time, and through him and in him all are preserved. To him of strongest faith Christ is nearest; and from him who least believes, is salvation farthest, so far as personal possession of it goes. Paul's reference here is to nearness of the revelation of salvation. When Christ came the promise was fulfilled. The Gospel was revealed to the world. Through Christ's coming it was publicly preached to all men. In recognition of these things, the apostle says: "Salvation is nearer to us" than when unrevealed and unfulfilled in the promise. In Titus 2:11, it is said, "For the grace of God hath appeared, bringing salvation." In other words, God's grace is revealed and publicly proclaimed; though the saints who lived prior to its manifestation nevertheless possessed it.

So the Scriptures teach the coming of Christ, notwithstanding he was already present to the fathers. However, he was not publicly proclaimed to mankind until after his resurrection from the dead. It is of this coming in the Gospel the Scriptures for the most part teach. Incident to this revelation he came in human form. The taking upon himself of humanity would have profited no one had it not meant the proclamation of the Gospel. The Gospel was to present him to the whole world, revealing the fact that he became man for the sake of imparting the blessing to all who, accepting the Gospel, should believe in him. Paul tells us (Rom. 1:2) the Gospel was promised of God; from which we may infer God placed more emphasis upon the Gospel, the public revelation of Christ through the Word, than upon his physical birth, his advent in human form. God's purpose was concerning the Gospel and our faith, and he permitted his Son to assume humanity for the sake of making possible the preaching of the Gospel of Christ; that through the revealed Word salvation in Christ might be brought near—might come—to all the world.

Some have presented four different forms of Christ's advent, adapted to the four Sundays in Advent. But the most vital form of his coming, that upon which all efficacy depends, the coming to which Paul here refers, they have failed to recognize. They know not what constitutes the Gospel, nor for what purpose it was given. Despite their much talk about the advent of Christ, they thrust him from us farther than heaven is from earth. How can Christ profit us unless he be embraced by faith? But how can he be embraced by faith where the Gospel is not preached?

THE DAY OF GRACE

"The night is far spent, and the day is at hand."

THIS IS EQUIVALENT to saying "salvation is near to us." By the word "day" Paul means the Gospel; the Gospel is like day in that it enlightens the heart or soul. Now, day having broken, salvation is near to us. In other words, Christ and his grace, promised to Abraham, are now revealed; they are preached in all the world, enlightening mankind, awakening us from sleep and making manifest the true, eternal blessings, that we may occupy ourselves with the Gospel of Christ and walk honorably in the day. By the word "night" we are to understand all doctrines apart from the Gospel. For there is no other saving doctrine; all else is night and darkness.

Notice carefully Paul's words. He designates the most beautiful and vivifying time of the day—the delightful, joyous dawn, the hour of sunrise. Then the night has passed and the day broken. In response to the morning dawn, birds sing, beasts arouse themselves and all humanity arises. At daybreak, when the sky is red in the east, the world is apparently new and all things reanimated. In many places in the Scriptures, the comforting, vivifying preaching of the Gospel is compared to the morning dawn, to the rising of the sun; sometimes the figure is implied and sometimes plainly expressed, as here where Paul styles the Gospel the breaking day. Again, Psalm 110:3, "Thy people offer themselves willingly in the day of thy power, in holy array: out of the womb of the morning thou hast the dew of thy youth." Here the Gospel is plainly denominated the womb of the morning, the day of Christ's power, wherein, as the dew is born of the morning, we are conceived and born children of Christ; and by no work of man, but from heaven and through the Holy Spirit's grace.

This Gospel day is produced by the glorious Sun Jesus Christ. Hence Malachi calls him the Sun of Righteousness, saying, "But unto you that fear my name shall the Sun of Righteousness arise with healing in its wings" (Mal. 4:2). All believers in Christ receive the light of his grace, and righteousness, and shall rejoice in the shelter of his wings. Again in Psalm 118:24, we read, "This is the day which Jehovah hath made; we will rejoice and be glad in it." The meaning is: The natural sun makes the natural day, but the Lord himself is the author of the spiritual day. Christ is the Sun, the source of the Gospel day. From him the Gospel brightness shines throughout the world. John 9:5 reads, "I am the light of the world."

Psalm 19:1 beautifully describes Christ the Sun, and the Gospel day, "The heavens declare the glory of God." As the natural heavens bring the sun and the day, and the sun is in the heavens, so the apostles in their preaching possess and bring to us the real Sun, Christ. The Psalm continues,

> "In them hath he set a tabernacle for the sun, which is as a bridegroom coming out of his chamber, and rejoiceth as a strong man to run his course. His going forth is from the end of the heavens, and his circuit unto the ends of it; and there is nothing hid from the heat thereof."

It all refers to the beautiful daybreak of the Gospel. Scripture sublimely exalts the Gospel day, for it is the source of life, joy, pleasure and energy, and brings all good. Hence the name "Gospel"—joyful news.

Who can enumerate the things revealed to us by this day—by the Gospel? It teaches us everything—the nature of God, of ourselves, and what has been and is to be in regard to heaven, hell and earth, to angels and devils. It enables us to know how to conduct ourselves in relation to these—whence we are and whither we go. But, being deceived by the devil, we forsake the light of day and seek to find truth among philosophers and heathen totally ignorant of such matters. In permitting ourselves to be blinded by human doctrines, we return to the night. Whatsoever is not the Gospel day surely cannot be light. Otherwise Paul, and in fact all Scripture, would not urge that day upon us and pronounce everything else night.

Our disposition to run counter to the perfectly plain teachings of Scripture and seek inferior light, when the Lord declares himself the Light and Sun of the world, must result from our having incurred the displeasure of Providence. Had we no other evidence that the high schools of the Pope are the devil's abominable fostering-places of harlots and knaves, the fact is amply plain in the way they shamelessly introduce and extol Aristotle, the inferior light, exercising themselves in him more than in Christ; rather they exercise themselves wholly in Aristotle and not at all in Christ.

"Let us therefore cast off the works of darkness, and let us put on the armor of light."

As Christ is the Sun and the Gospel is the day, so faith is the light, or the seeing and watching on that day. We are not profited by the shining of the sun, and the day it produces, if our eyes fail to perceive its light. Similarly, though the Gospel is revealed, and proclaims Christ to the world, it enlightens none but those who receive it, who have risen from sleep through the agency of the light of faith. They who sleep are not affected by the sun and the day; they receive no light therefrom, and see as little as if there were neither sun nor day. It is to our day Paul refers when he says, "Dear brethren, knowing the season, that already it is time for you to awake out of sleep, etc." Though the hour is one of spiritual opportunity, it has been revealed in secular time, and is daily being revealed. In the light of our spiritual knowledge we are to rise from sleep and lay aside the works of darkness. Thus it is plain Paul is not addressing unbelievers. As before said, he is not here teaching the doctrine of faith, but its works and fruits. He tells the Romans they know the time is at hand, that the night is past and the day has broken.

Do you ask, Why this passage to believers? As already stated, preaching is twofold in character: it may teach or it may incite and exhort. No one ever gets to the point of knowledge where it is not necessary to admonish him—continually to urge him—to new reflections upon what he already knows; for there is danger of his untiring enemies—the devil, the world and the flesh—wearying him and causing him to become negligent, and ultimately lulling him to sleep. Peter says (1 Pet. 5:8), "Your adversary the devil, as a roaring lion, walketh about, seeking whom he may devour." In consequence of this fact, he says, "Be sober, be watchful." Similarly Paul's thought here is that since the devil, the world and the flesh cease not to assail us, there should be continuous exhorting and impelling to vigilance and activity. Hence the Holy Spirit is called the "Paraclete," the Comforter or Helper, who incites and urges to good.

Hence Paul's appropriate choice of words. Not the works of darkness but the works of light he terms "armor." And why "armor" rather than "works"? Doubtless to teach that only at the cost of conflicts, pain, labor and danger will the truly watchful and godly life be maintained; for these three powerful enemies, the devil, the world and the flesh, unceasingly oppose us day and night. Hence Job (7:1) regards the life of man on earth as a life of trial and warfare.

Now, it is no easy thing to stand always in battle array during the whole of life. Good trumpets and bugles are necessary preaching and exhortation of the sort to enable us valiantly to maintain our position in battle. Good works are armor: evil works are not; unless, indeed, we submit and give them control over us. Then they likewise become armor. Paul says, "Neither present your members unto sin as instruments of unrighteousness" (Rom. 6:13), meaning: Let not the works of darkness get such control of you as to render your members weapons of unrighteousness.

Now, as already made plain, the word "light" here carries the thought of "faith." The light of faith, in the Gospel day, shines from Christ the Sun into our hearts. The armor of light, then, is simply the works of faith. On the other hand, "darkness" is unbelief; it reigns in the absence of the Gospel and of Christ, through the instrumentality of the doctrines of men—of human reason—instigated by the devil. The "works of darkness" are, therefore, the "works of unbelief." As Christ is Lord and Ruler in the realm of that illuminating faith, so, as Paul says (Eph. 6:12), the devil is ruler of this darkness; that is, over unbelievers. For he says again (2 Cor. 4:3-4),

> "And even if our gospel is veiled, it is veiled in them that perish: in whom the god of this world [that is, the devil] hath blinded the minds of the unbelieving, that the light of the gospel of the glory of Christ . . . should not dawn upon them."

The character of the two kinds of works, however, will be discussed later.

"Let us walk, becomingly (honestly), as in the day."

Works of darkness are not wrought in the day. Fear of being shamed before men makes one conduct himself honorably. The proverbial expression "shameless night" is a true one. Works we are ashamed to perform in the day are wrought in the night. The day, being shamefaced, constrains us to walk honorably. A Christian should so live that he need never be ashamed of the character of his works, though they be revealed to all the world. He whose life and conduct are such as to make him unwilling his deeds should be manifest to everyone, certainly does not live in a Christian manner. In this connection Christ says,

> "For everyone that doeth evil hateth the light, and cometh not to the light, lest his works should be reproved. But he that doeth the truth

cometh to the light, that his works may be made manifest, that they have been wrought in God" (John 3:20-21).

So you see the urgent necessity for inciting and exhorting to be vigilant and to put on the armor of light. How many Christians now could endure the revelation of all their works to the light of day? What kind of Christian life do we hypocrites lead if we cannot endure the exposure of our conduct before men, when it is now exposed to God, his angels and creatures, and on the last day shall be revealed to all? A Christian ought to live as he would be found in the last day before all men. "Walk as children of light, for the fruit of the light is in all goodness and righteousness and truth" (Eph. 5:9). "Take thought for things honorable," not only in the sight of God, but also "in the sight of all men" (Rom. 12:17). "For our glorying is this, the testimony of our conscience, that in holiness and sincerity of God, not in fleshly wisdom . . . we behaved ourselves in the world" (2 Cor. 1:12).

But such a life certainly cannot be maintained in the absence of faith, when faith itself—vigilant, active, valiant faith—has enough to do to remain constant, sleepless and unwearied. Essential as it is that doctrine be preached to the illiterate, it is just as essential to exhort the learned not to fall from their incipient right living, under the assaults of raging flesh, subtle world and treacherous devil.

"Not in revelling and drunkenness, not in chambering and wantonness, not in strife and jealousy."

Here Paul enumerates certain works of darkness. In the beginning of the discourse he alludes to one as "sleep." In 1 Thessalonians 5:6, it is written: "Let us not sleep, as do the rest, but let us watch and be sober." Not that the apostle warns against physical sleep; he means spiritual sleep—unbelief, productive of the works of darkness. Yet physical sleep may likewise be an evil work when indulged in from lust and revelling, through indolence and excessive inebriety, to the obstruction of light and the weakening of the armor of light. These six works of darkness include all others, such as are enumerated in Galatians 5:19-21, and Colossians 3:5 and 8. We will divide them into two general classes, the right hand class and the left hand class. Upon the right are arrayed these four—revelling, drunkenness, chambering and wantonness; on the left, strife and jealousy. For scripturally, the left side signifies adversity and its attendant evils—wrath, jealousy, and so on. The right side stands for prosperity and its results—rioting, drunkenness, lust, indolence, and the like.

Plainly, then, Paul means to include under the two mentioned works of darkness—strife and jealousy—all of similar character. For instance, the things enumerated in Ephesians 4:31, which says, "Let all bitterness, and wrath, and anger, and clamor, and railing, be put away from you, with all malice"; and again in Galatians 5:19-21, reading, "Now the works of the flesh are . . . enmities, strife, jealousies, wraths, factions, divisions, parties, envyings, drunkenness, revellings and such like." In short, "strife and jealousy" here stand for innumerable evils resulting from wrath, be it in word or deed.

Likewise under the four vices—revelling, drunkenness, indolence and lewdness—the apostle includes all the vices of unchastity in word or deed, things none would wish to enumerate. The six works mentioned suffice to teach that he who lives in the darkness of unbelief does not keep himself pure in his neighbor's sight, but is immoderate in all his conduct, toward himself and toward his fellow-man. Further comment on these words is unnecesary. Everyone knows the meaning of "revelling and drunkenness"—excessive eating and drinking, more for the gratification of appetite than for nourishment of the body. Again, it is not hard to understand the reference to idleness in bed-chambers, to lewdness and unchasity. The apostle's words stand for the indulgence of the lusts and appetites of the flesh: excessive sleeping and indolence; every form of unchastity and sensuality practiced by the satiated, indolent and stupid, in daytime or nighttime, in retirement or elsewhere, privately or publicly—vices that seek material darkness and secret places. These vices Paul terms "chambering and wantonness." And the meaning of "strife" and of "jealousy" is generally understood.

PUT ON CHRIST, THE ARMOR OF LIGHT

"But put ye on the Lord Jesus Christ."

IN THIS ADMONITION to put on Christ, Paul briefly prescribes all the armor of light. Christ is "put on" in two ways. First, we may clothe ourselves with his virtues. This is effected through the faith that relies on the fact of Christ having in his death accomplished all for us. For not our righteousness, but the righteousness of Christ, reconciled us to God and redeemed us from sin. This manner of putting on Christ is treated of in the doctrine concerning faith; it gives Christ to us as a gift and a pledge. Relative to this topic more will be said in the epistle for New Year's day, Galatians 3:27, "For as many of you as were baptized into Christ did put on Christ."

Secondly, Christ being our example and pattern, whom we are to follow and copy, clothing ourselves in the virtuous garment of his walk, Paul fittingly says we should "put on" Christ. As expressed in 1 Corinthians 15:49, "As we have borne the image of the earthy, we shall also bear the image of the heavenly." And again (Eph. 4:22-24),

> "That ye put away, as concerning your former manner of life, the old man, that waxeth corrupt after the lusts of deceit; and that ye be renewed in the spirit of your mind, and put on the new man, that after God hath been created in righteousness and holiness of truth."

Now, in Christ we behold only the true armor of light. No gormandizing or drunkenness is here; nothing but fasting, moderation, and restraint of the flesh, incident to labor, exertion, preaching, praying and doing good to mankind. No indolence, apathy or unchastity exists, but true discipline, purity, vigilance, early rising. The fields are couch for him who has neither house, chamber, nor bed. With him is no wrath, strife or envying; rather utter goodness, love, mercy, patience. Paul presents Christ the example in a few words where he says (Col. 3:12-15),

> "Put on therefore, as God's elect, holy and beloved, a heart of compassion, kindness, lowliness, meekness, longsuffering; forbearing

one another, and forgiving each other, if any man have a complaint against any, even as the Lord forgave you, so also do ye: and above all these things put on love, which is the bond of perfectness, and let the peace of Christ rule in your hearts, to the which also ye were called in one body; and be ye thankful."

Again, in Philippians 2:5-8, after commanding his flock to love and serve one another, he presents as an example the same Christ who became servant unto us. He says,

"Have this mind in you, which was also in Christ Jesus: who, existing in the form of God, counted not the being on an equality with God a thing to be grasped, but emptied himself, taking the form of a servant, being made in the likeness of men; and being found in fashion as a man."

Now, the armor of light is, briefly, the good works opposed to gluttony, drunkenness, licentiousness; to indolence, strife and envying: such as fasting, watchfulness, prayer, labor, chastity, modesty, temperance, goodness, endurance of hunger and thirst, of cold and heat. Not to employ my own words, let us hear Paul's enumeration of good works in Galatians 5:22-23, "The fruit of the Spirit is love, joy, peace, longsuffering, kindness, goodness, faithfulness, meekness, self-control." But he makes a still more comprehensive count in 2 Corinthians 6:1-10,

"We entreat also that ye receive not the grace of God in vain (for he saith, At an acceptable time I hearkened unto thee, and in a day of salvation did I succor thee: behold, now is the acceptable time; behold, now is the day of salvation) [in other words, For now is salvation nearer to us than when we first believed, and now is the time to awake out of sleep]: giving no occasion of stumbling in anything, that our ministration be not blamed; but in everything commending ourselves, as ministers of God, in much patience, in afflictions, in necessities, in distresses, in stripes, in imprisonments, in tumults, in labors, in watchings, in fastings; in pureness, in knowledge, in longsuffering, in kindness, in the Holy Spirit, in love unfeigned, in the word of truth, in the power of God; by the armor of righteousness on the right hand and on the left, by glory and dishonor, by evil report and good report; as deceivers, and yet true; as unknown, and yet well known; as dying, and behold, we live; as chastened, and not killed; as sorrowful, yet always rejoicing; as poor, yet making many rich; as having nothing, and yet possessing all things."

What a rich stream of eloquence flows from Paul's lips! He makes plain enough in what consists the armor of light on the left hand and on the right. To practice these good works is truly putting on Jesus Christ.

It is a very beautiful feature in this passage that it presents the very highest example, the Lord himself, when it says, "Put ye on the Lord." Here is a strong incentive. For the individual who can see his master fasting, laboring, watching, enduring hunger and fatigue, while he himself feasts, idles, sleeps, and lives in luxury, must be a scoundrel. What master could tolerate such conduct in a servant? Or what servant would dare attempt such things? We can but blush with shame when we behold our unlikeness to Christ.

Who can influence to action him who refuses to be warmed and aroused by the example of Christ himself? What is to be accomplished by the rustling of leaves and the sound of words when the thunder-clap of Christ's example fails to move us? Paul was particular to add the word "Lord," saying, "Put ye on the Lord Jesus Christ." As if to say: "Ye servants, think not yourselves great and exalted. Look upon your Lord, who, though under no obligation, denied himself."

"And make not provision for the flesh, to fulfil the lusts thereof."

Paul here briefly notices two different provisions for the flesh. One is supplying its natural wants—furnishing the body with food and raiment necessary to sustain life and vigor; guarding against enfeebling it and unfitting it for labor by too much restraint.

The other provision is a sinful one, the gratification of the lusts and inordinate appetites. This Paul here forbids. It is conducive to works of darkness. The flesh must be restrained and made subservient to the spirit. It must not dismount its master, but carry him if necessary. Sirach (33:24) says, "Fodder, a wand, and burdens are for the ass; and bread, correction, and work for a servant." He does not say the animal is to be mistreated or maimed; nor does he say the servant is to be abused or imprisoned. Thus to the body pertains subjection, labor and whatever is essential to its proper welfare. Paul says of himself: "I buffet my body, and bring it into bondage [subjection]" (1 Cor. 9:27). He does not say he brings his body to illness or death, but makes it serve in submission to the spirit.

Paul adds this last admonition for the sake of two classes of people. One class is represented by them who make natural necessity an excuse to indulge their lusts and gratify their desires. Because of humanity's proneness to such error, many saints, deploring the sin, have often in the attempt to resist it, unduly restrained their bodies. So subtle and deceptive is nature in the matter of its demands and its lusts, no man can wholly handle it; he must live this life in insecurity and concern.

The other class is represented by the blind saints who imagine the kingdom of God and his righteousness are dependent upon the particular meat and drink, clothing and couch, of their own choice. They look no farther than at their individual work in this respect, and fancy that in fasting until the brain is disordered, the stomach deranged or the body emaciated, they have done well. Upon this subject Paul says (1 Cor. 8:8), "Food will not commend us to God; neither, if we eat not, are we the worse; nor, if we eat, are we the better." Again (Col. 2:18-23),

> "Let no man rob you of your prize by a voluntary humility and worshipping of the angels . . . which things have indeed a show of wisdom in will-worship, and humility, and severity to the body; but are not of any value against the indulgence of the flesh."

Gerson commended the Carthusians for not eating meat, even though debility made meat a necessity. He would deny it even at the cost of life. Thus was the great man deceived by this superstitious, angelic spirituality. What if God judges its votaries as murderers of themselves? Indeed, no orders, statutes or vows contrary to the command of God can rightfully be made; and if made they would profit no more than would a vow to break one's marriage contract. Certainly God has here in the words of Paul forbidden such destruction of our own bodies. It is our duty to allow the body all necessary food, whether wine, meat, eggs or anything else; whether the time be Friday, Sunday, in Lent or after the feast of Easter; regardless of all orders, traditions and vows, and of the Pope. No prohibition contrary to God's command can avail, though made by the angels even.

This wretched folly of vows has its rise in darkness and blindness; the looking upon mere works and trusting to be saved by the number and magnitude of them. Paul would make of works "armor of light," and employ them to overcome the works of darkness. Thus far, then, and no farther, should fasting, vigilance and exertion be practiced. Before God it matters not at all whether you eat fish or meat, drink water or wine, wear red or green, do this or that. All foods are good creations of God and to be used. Only take heed to be temperate in appropriating them and to abstain when it is necessary to the conquest of the works of darkness. It is impossible to lay down a common rule of abstinence, for all bodies are not constituted alike. One needs more, another less. Everyone must judge for himself, and must care for his body according to the advice of Paul: "Make not provision for the flesh, to fulfil the lusts thereof." Had there been any other rule for us, Paul would not have omitted it here.

Hence, you see, the ecclesiastical traditions that flatly forbid the eating of meat are contrary to the Gospel. Paul predicts their appearance in 1 Timothy 4:1-3, where he says,

> "But the Spirit saith expressly, that in later times some shall fall away from the faith, giving heed to seducing spirits and doctrines of demons, through the hypocrisy of men that speak lies, branded in their own conscience as with a hot iron; forbidding to marry, and commanding to abstain from meats, which God created to be received with thanksgiving."

That these words have reference to ecclesiastical orders and those of the entire Papacy, no one can deny. They are plain. Hence the nature of Roman Catholic works is manifest.

Also you will note here Paul does not sanction the fanatical devotion of certain effeminate saints who set apart to themselves particular days for fasting, as a special service to God, one for this saint, another for that. These are all blind paths, leading us to base our blessings on works. Without distinction of days and meats, our lives should be temperate and sober throughout. If good works are to be our armor of light, and if the entire life is to be pure and chaste, we must never lay off the arms of defense, but always be found sober, temperate, vigilant, energetic. These fanatical saints, however, fast one day on bread and water and then eat and drink to excess every day for one-fourth of the year. Again, some fast from food in the evening but drink immoderately. And who can mention all the folly and works of darkness originating from regarding works for the sake of the efforts themselves and not for the purpose they serve. Men convert the armor of good works into a mirror, fasting without knowing the reason for abstinence. They are like those who bear a sword merely to look at, and when assailed do not use it. This is enough on today's epistle lesson.

2
Second Sunday in Advent

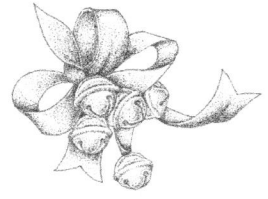

"For whatsoever things were written aforetime were written for our learning, that through patience and through comfort of the scriptures we might have hope. Now the God of patience and of comfort grant you to be of the same mind one with another according to Christ Jesus: that with one accord ye may with one mouth glorify the God and Father of our Lord Jesus Christ. Wherefore receive ye one another, even as Christ also received you, to the glory of God. For I say that Christ hath been made a minister of the circumcision for the truth of God, that he might confirm the promises given unto the fathers, and that the Gentiles might glorify God for his mercy; as it is written,

Therefore will I give praise unto thee among the Gentiles, And sing unto thy name.

And again he saith, Rejoice, ye Gentiles, with his people.

And again, Praise the Lord, all ye Gentiles;

And let all the peoples praise him.

And again, Isaiah saith, There shall be the root of Jesse,

And he that ariseth to rule over the Gentiles;

On him shall the Gentiles hope.

Now the God of hope fill you with all joy and peace in believing, that ye may abound in hope, in the power of the Holy Spirit" (Romans 15:4-13).

EXHORTATION TO BEAR WITH THE WEAK

IT IS QUITE PROBABLE the individual who arranged this epistle text knew little about Paul. He includes in the selection more than pertains to the theme. The beginning—"Whatsoever things were written," etc.—relates to what goes before. The text should have begun with the words, "Now the God of patience." It is necessary to a clear and methodical understanding of the passage that we remember this: the Romans to whom the apostle writes were converts to Christianity from both Jews and gentiles. At that time there were many Jews living in all countries, and especially were they found in Rome, as we learn from the seventeenth and eighteenth chapters of the Acts of the Apostles. Having properly inculcated the doctrines of faith and of good works all through the epistle, the apostle in conclusion introduces several exhortations to the Romans to preserve harmony in faith and in good works, removing what might be productive of discord and subversive to unity of the Spirit. There are two difficulties which today as in all times strongly militate against the unity of the Spirit, against faith and good works. They must here be carefully noted and described.

The first difficulty was this: Some Jewish converts feared that deviating from former customs would be committing sin. Notwithstanding they had been taught the New Testament freedom regarding meats, days, clothing, vessels, persons, conditions, customs; that only faith renders us righteous in God's sight; and that the restrictions of the Law concerning the eating of flesh and fish, concerning holidays, places, vessels, were entirely abolished; yet so completely fettered by old customs were their weak consciences and imperfect faith, they could not exercise such liberties. Again, both Jews and gentiles, in consequence of this same disordered idea, could not venture to eat of bread and meat offered to idols by unbelievers, though sold in the public market. They imagined that to eat thereof was to honor the idols and deny Christ, when in fact the act had no significance. For all kinds of food are clean, and good creatures of God, whether in the hands of heathen or Christians, whether offered to God or to the devil.

The second difficulty was this: They of better understanding and stronger faith had not sufficient regard for the weak, but exercised their liberty indiscreetly, offending the weak by eating and drinking without discrimination whatever was set before them. Not that there was any wrong in the act so far as the food was concerned; the wrong consisted in their indiscretion in causing the weak to err through the act. For the latter, beholding, could neither agree with them nor dissent from them. Had they thought to consent, their weak consciences would have interposed, protesting, "It is sinful; do it not." Had they thought to dissent, conscience again would have interposed, objecting, "You are not Christians for you do not as other Christians do; your faith must be false." Thus they could neither do one thing nor the other without opposing conscience. Now, to violate conscience is equivalent to violating faith, and is a grievous sin.

Paul here teaches us to have patience and bear with the weak, and not to conduct ourselves carelessly before them; rather to agree with them—become weak with them—until they grow stronger in the faith and recognize their liberty. We are to guard against creating discord in faith over the subject of meats and drinks or any other temporal thing.

The apostle, however, discriminates upon this point, for in general his teaching recognizes two classes of individuals to be considered in the matter. One consists of those weak in the faith, of whom we have already spoken. It is to this class alone Paul here refers. They are good, pious, common people, willingly doing better when they have the knowledge or power. They are not tenacious of their opinions; the trouble lies altogether in weakness of conscience and lack of faith. They are unable to extricate themselves from prevailing doctrines and customs. The other class are obstinate. Not satisfied to enjoy liberty of conduct for themselves, they must enforce it upon others, constraining them to their own practices. They claim that because certain liberty is permissible, it must be enjoined. They will not listen to real truth in the matter of Christian liberty, but strive against it. They are to blame for the weakness of the first class. For their doctrine disregards the weak consciences and misleads them into the belief that certain conduct is essential. This domineering class delight in bringing simple consciences into subjection to their demands. Paul does not here refer to that manner of people; no, but he elsewhere teaches us to faithfully oppose them and always do the opposite (Titus 1).

The best rule to follow in such matters is the rule of love. You should hold the same attitude toward these two classes that you would toward a wolf and a sheep. Suppose a wolf were to wound almost fatally a sheep, and you were to proceed with rage against the sheep, declaring it to be wrong in being wounded, that it should be sound; and you were violently to compel it to follow the other sheep to the pasture and to the fold, giving it no special care; would not all men declare you inconsiderate? The sheep might well say: "Certainly it is wrong for me to be wounded, and unquestionably I ought to be sound; but direct your anger toward the inflicter of my wounds, and assist in my recovery." So should these Romans have done and have faithfully repelled the wolf-like teachers. At the same time, the consciences weakened and discouraged by false doctrines should have received consideration. The Church at Rome ought not to have denounced nor ignored them, but rather to have carefully healed their spiritual disorder and ultimately eradicated the wrong doctrines, in patience bearing with their weak brethren lest they should cause them to err.

Now, the circumstance Paul here speaks of has long since passed, and the law of Moses concerning meats, drinks, apparel, place, and so on, is no longer pertinent; yet another has been introduced in its stead, causing even greater trouble, and Paul's doctrine on this point is more necessary now than then. There is today established by the Pope and the clergy a world-wide system of human devices in regard to meats and drinks, apparel and place, days and seasons, persons and orders, customs and performances, so elaborate that one can scarce eat a morsel, drink a drop, or open his eyes even, but there is a law concerning the act. Thus is our liberty usurped. Particularly is it true in convents and cloisters, where it is unanimously contended that we must be clothed and shorn in a certain way, must conduct ourselves by certain rules, and must not eat this meat, drink that drink, and so on, lest we sin by disobedience. There obedience to human doctrines has been exalted to the point of highest esteem. The monks and nuns regard it the foundation, the corner-stone, of their religion, and base upon it their souls' salvation.

No one will open his eyes to the fact that mere human devices and doctrines are ensnaring souls, weakening consciences, dissipating Christian liberty and faith, and replenishing hell. Wolves! Wolves! How abominably, awfully, murderous, how harassing and destructive, are these things the world over! This matter of obedience to human doctrine has never been agitated sufficiently to discover weak consciences. No one has opposed in word or act the teachings harmful to them. Whosoever has deviated from the doctrines has been condemned, and denounced as an apostate, a roving monk, an abandoned Christian. Thus forcibly have the sheep not only been enfeebled, but driven into the jaws of the wolf. Oh, the wrath, the indignation, the displeasure, of the Divine Majesty!

If now, by the mercy of God, these Roman Catholic doctrines should be recognized as merely human, as false and assumed, things God has not commanded; and if some were to have courage enough to depart from custom in the matter of masses, prayers, garb, meats, and to maintain their Christian liberty according to the Gospel, the two classes referred to would take offense. The first, the Catholics, would rant and rage, making loud outcry: "Our teachings must be observed! He who disregards them is a heretic, a heathen, a Jew, and disobedient to the Church." They would continue to cry "Obedience to the Church!" solely for the sake of retaining in fetters and spiritual death the consciences which, as they have been taught to do, regard their obedience as unto the Church, when in reality it is unto mere Roman Catholic knavery and satanic devices, things whereby many saints, even, have been misled and deceived; St. Francis, for instance, and others.

The second class—the weak—in the face of the others' outcry and of their own established custom, would err, being puzzled as to whose doctrine to accept, though sincerely desirous to follow the right. But whatever course they might take, conscience would oppose them. Should they essay to accept our Christian liberty, their own established custom and the outcry of the Catholics would deter them. Their consciences bound by these two restraints, they would not dare deviate from the old way lest they oppose God. On the other hand, should they not accept our Christian liberty, they would again fear they were opposing the God we proclaim. Whither, then, shall flee the poor, weak conscience over whom Christ and the devil contend?

To this situation Paul's teaching appropriately applies. The doctrine of the devil and his Catholics is wholly destitute of compassion. In violent rage it compels immediate retraction from our doctrine of liberty. It excommunicates and curses the offender, casting him down four thousand miles below hell, if he does not recant in the twinkling of an eye and renounce every letter and tittle of his belief. From the fact of the rage manifested, as well as from the fruit of Roman Catholic doctrine, we perceive who is its author. The teaching of Christ, however, does not so. It calls not for summary rejection of the individual who fails to quickly retract and readily desist when found to err in faith; notwithstanding there is more reason it should than in the case of papal teaching. Recognizing the weak and wounded condition of the offender, Christ's doctrine comes in a friendly way, teaching the real truth about human laws—that of Christian liberty. It is patient, bearing with him who does not immediately abandon his erroneous ways, and giving him time to learn to forsake them. It allows him to do the best he can, according to what he has been used to, until he is made whole and clearly perceives the truth.

Therefore, the Christian must on this point discriminate between the two classes mentioned. The weak should receive his kindly and patient instruction, but the roving, ranting kind are to meet with his earnest opposition. Let him teach and perform everything calculated to annoy and oppose the latter, and quietly omit whatever is pleasing to them, and let him honor their ban with a great easel-box. This is the consistent course of Christian love. It is the treatment every man desires for himself. Were any one of us misled by a weak conscience, he would desire a little time to retrieve instead of being precipitately cut off from the Church. He would like to be kindly instructed, to be borne with for a while and to be delivered from the wolves. Such is Christ's conduct toward us, and such does he desire our conduct toward one another to be.

The second cause of discord Paul also removes. There is, and always will be, among Christ's followers a class who are weak and sickly in good works, just as the first were defective in faith. We have, then, two kinds of invalid Christians—those affected inwardly, in faith and conscience; and those outwardly unsound, in works and deportment. Christ desires none of them to be rejected, but would have all received.

He would give Christian love abundant opportunity to exercise itself, to heal its neighbors, to do them good and to bear with them, in matters inward and outward—in faith and conduct. The weak in conduct are they who sometimes fall into open sin; or again they who are called in German "wunderliche Koepfe und Seltsame," people easily irritated or with other shortcomings which make it difficult to get along with them. Especially have we instances among husbands and wives, masters and servants, rulers and subjects.

Now, where Paul's Christian doctrine does not obtain, naturally each individual forgets the beam in his own eye and perceives only the mote in his neighbor's. One will not bear with the faults of the other; each requires perfection of his fellow. Hence they reflect upon each other's conduct. One resorts to this subterfuge, the other to that, to evade the harassing censure and displeasure of his neighbor. He who can, cuts the other's acquaintance, drops him, and then justifies himself with the excuse that his motive was love of righteousness; that he did not want to associate with wicked persons, but desired the company of only the good and godly like himself.

This evil holds sway chiefly in individuals ranking more or less high in the estimation of their fellows, who lead respectable lives and are particularly favored. These puff themselves up and put on airs. Whoever is not just like them is held in disgrace, in disparagement and contempt. Only themselves are worthy of admiration. But he who measures up to them, whose life is equally respectable—ah! he is righteous and a good friend; with him they can associate with perfect satisfaction to themselves as individuals who love only righteousness and the righteous, and hate nothing but wickedness and the wicked. They are not aware of the secret satanical pride in the inmost recesses of their hearts, which pride is the very reason they haughtily and meanly despise their neighbors for their imperfections.

Love of virtue and hatred of vice may spring from two different motives; one heathenish, the other Christian. Christ, too, is an enemy to sin and a friend to righteousness. Psalms 45:7 says of him, "Thou hast loved righteousness, and hated wickedness." And this saying does not conflict with Moses' declaration concerning Christ, "Dilexit populos," "Yea, he loveth the people" (Deut. 33:3). But heathen love of virtue and hatred of vice, like the unreasoning swine, indiscriminately roots up and tosses together vices and virtues, regardless of the individual; truly a friend to no one but itself. This truth is evident from the fact that so long and so far as virtue adorns the individual, so long and so far heathenism loves him and is interested in him; but when virtue is lacking, the individual is rejected.

Now, the Christian hatred of sin discriminates between the vices and the individual. It endeavors to exterminate only the former and to preserve the latter. It does not flee from, evade, reject nor despise anyone; rather it receives every man, takes a warm interest in him and accords him treatment calculated to relieve him of his vices. It admonishes, instructs and prays for him. It patiently bears with him. It does only as the doer would be done by in circumstances of like infirmities.

The Christian's whole purpose in life is to be useful to mankind; not to cast out the individual, but to exterminate his vices. This we cannot do if we refuse to tolerate the faulty person. It would be a very inconsistent case of charity in which you should desire to feed the hungry, satisfy the thirsty, clothe the naked, visit the sick, but at the same time should not permit the hungering, the thirsting, the naked and the sick to approach you. But just so your unwillingness to tolerate a wicked or faulty person is inconsistent with your willingness to help him, or to aid him to godly living.

Let us learn from this that the life of Christian love does not consist in seeking godly, upright, holy individuals, but in making them godly, upright and holy. Let this be the Christian's earthly labor, whether it calls for admonition, prayer, patience or other exercise. For the Christian does not live to seek after the wealthy and strong in virtue, but to make such virtuous ones from the poor, weak and infirm.

So, then, the text admonishes to two thoughts—to Christian love and to good and noble works; not only to bearing with our neighbor's spiritual imperfections of faith and conduct, but also to receiving him into fellowship, to healing him and to restoring from infirmities. They who fail so to do, create seditions, sects and divisions; as in time past the heretics, Donatists and Novatians, and many others, separated from the Church because unwilling to tolerate sinners and the faulty. There must be heretics and sects where the doctrine of Christian love is ignored; it cannot be otherwise.

St. Augustine, commenting on the sixth chapter of Galatians, says,

> "In nothing is one's religious character so well shown as when, in dealing with the sinful individual, he insists on redemption of the sinner rather than on reproach; on his welfare rather than on reproof."

Upon this subject of Christian love, Paul says (Gal. 6:1-2),

> "Brethren, even if a man be overtaken in any trespass, ye who are spiritual, restore such a one in a spirit of gentleness; looking to thyself, lest thou also be tempted. Bear ye one another's burdens, and so fulfill the law of Christ."

In other words: "Neglect not to take upon yourselves the burdens of your neighbor—whatever is hard for him to bear. Seek not to derive advantage from him, but bear his burdens." To use him for your own advantage is not bearing but being borne. Advantage belongs to the angels in yonder life. At the same time we are to make a distinction between the two classes before mentioned. We are to avoid as heathen those who obstinately attempt to justify their sins and are unwilling to forsake them. For so we are taught in Matthew 18:17. The doctrine of Christian love is applicable only to them who, though perceiving the wrong, yet stumble through weakness or imperfection. Let us examine the text.

THE WORD OF HOPE

"For whatsoever things were written aforetime were written for our learning, that through patience and through comfort of the Scriptures we might have hope."

IN THE SELECTION of this epistle passage it should not have been made to begin with these words. They pertain to the first part of the chapter. We shall therefore present the text in its proper order. The apostle with the fifteenth chapter begins to teach the aforesaid principle of love which is to have expression in our attitude toward our neighbor of erring conduct; even as in the fourteenth chapter he taught us to manifest love toward our neighbor of imperfect faith. He says,

> "We that are strong ought to bear the infirmities of the weak, and not to please ourselves. Let each one of us please his neighbor for that which is good, unto edifying. For Christ also pleased not himself; but, as it is written, The reproaches of them that reproached thee fell upon me. For whatsoever things were written aforetime were written for our learning, that through patience and through comfort of the scriptures we might have hope."

In these truly forcible words Paul teaches the principle of love that is to enable us to bear with the imperfect conduct of our neighbor.

First, he tells us we are under obligation to forbear. Whence arises this obligation? Doubtless from the Law and from love (Matt. 7:12), "All things whatsoever ye would that men should do unto you, even so do ye also unto them; for this is the law and the prophets." Now, there is no one of us who would not have others bear with him in his infirmities and help him to do better. In return, we are under obligation to conduct ourselves in a similar manner toward our fellows. The strong should bear with the feeble and help them to better things.

Secondly, Paul teaches we are not to take pleasure in ourselves; that is, not to consider ourselves good because of abilities superior to those of our neighbors. For that means but to delight in beholding others in sin and depravity, from unwillingness to see them our equals or our superiors; and to rejoice at the misfortunes which prevent their gaining ascendancy. Truly this spirit is diametrically and fundamentally opposed to love. The Pharisee in the Gospel (Luke 18:11) thanks God he is not like other men. So good does he regard himself and so does he delight in himself, it would be painful indeed to him were there any other without sin.

Now, are not they detestable individuals who begrudge grace and salvation to others, and who rejoice to see them ruined in sin, but at the same time are ambitious to be regarded pious and holy, strong enemies to sin and friends to godliness? But what is Paul's teaching? Emphatically not this. He says no one should unduly approve himself—regard himself good. What then? Let him secure the approbation of others. Let everyone so conduct himself as to gain the approval of his neighbor. Each should bear his neighbor's infirmities with patience and gentleness, and by kindness win his love and confidence. Let him not treat his neighbor with a rashness and severity that shall warrant the latter's fear and shall drive him farther away, leading him to expect no favors ever and to become but more sinful.

But you will say, "If I proceed in the way that shall please my neighbor I must let him have his own way and allow him to continue as he is." But this is not Paul's thought, for he adds the modifier "for his good." His meaning is that each should so conduct himself as to please his neighbor in the things that make for that neighbor's betterment, and in those only. And, indeed, our conduct toward our fellow may be such as to deny him his will without incurring his displeasure. But if he be dissolute beyond our power to benefit him, let him go; we have made a reasonable effort to gratify him in so far as we could contribute to his improvement. We cannot force his approval of our efforts to please him. Paul requires no more of us than to please our neighbor in the way of ministering to his good. The world does not delight even in the fact that God gave his own Son to die for its happiness.

Therefore, when Paul tells us everyone should please his neighbor in that which is good, his intent is not for us merely to strive to please our fellows; that is not what is required of us. But he would have us, in obedience to the rule of love, conduct ourselves in a way we might reasonably expect pleasing to them; in a way that if we fail we are not at fault. Paul says in 1 Corinthians 10:33: "Even as I also please all men in all things." So would he have us please everyone in all things? How did

Paul please all men when Jews and gentiles were his deadly enemies? He did everything for their benefit, and what reasonably should have pleased them.

Now, in the third place, to more effectually impress this doctrine, the apostle cites the example of Christ, saying Christ did not please himself. And what does he mean? Simply that notwithstanding Christ's holiness and graciousness, he did not despise us. Nor did he have pride in himself as the Pharisee did because he possessed something we had not. He rejoiced not in the fact that we had nothing while he had all things and all power. On the contrary, because he was grieved over our destitute condition, he devised a plan to be with us whereby we may become like him—possessing what he possesses and being liberated from our sins. There being no other way, he put forth his whole being and all his powers to accomplish our redemption. He assumed our sins and exterminated them. His purpose in it all was to please us and to win our affection. Thus is fulfilled Psalms 69:9, "The reproaches of them that reproach thee are fallen upon me." Our sins reproach and dishonor God, as our good conduct contributes to his honor and praise. So the prophet speaks of God's reproach and dishonor. All our sins are fallen upon Christ so as to be removed from us. Had Christ treated us as the Pharisee treated the publican, and as haughty saints do poor, faulty sinners, who of us would have been redeemed? Paul again holds up the example of Christ in Philippians 2:5-8,

> "Have this mind in you, which was also in Christ Jesus: who, existing in the form of God, counted not the being on an equality with God a thing to be grasped, but emptied himself, taking the form of a servant, being made in the likeness of men; and being found in fashion as a man, he humbled himself, becoming obedient even unto death, yea, the death of the cross."

Such should be our spirit in regard to the sins of our neighbor. We should not judge, backbite nor condemn him. We should keep an undesigning eye upon him, solely for the purpose of delivering him, even at the hazard of our own bodies, our lives, fortunes and honor. Let him who fails here, know he has lost Christ and is a heathen saint.

Now follows our text. It is because of the words cited from Psalm 69 concerning Christ that Paul says, "For whatsoever things were written aforetime," etc. By way of explaining the bearing of that passage here, and in what way it concerns us when it was spoken of Christ and is fulfilled in him, the apostle goes on to give us a general admonition from the Scriptures, saying that not only this passage but the entire Scriptures were written for our learning. True, the Bible contains much about Christ. But so it contains much about numerous saints—Adam, Abel, Noah, Abraham, Isaac, Jacob—which was not recorded for their sakes. The Bible was written long after their time; they never saw it.

So, however much is written about Christ, it is not for his sake; he had no need for it. It is recorded for our instruction. The record of Christ's words and deeds is for our edification, the model for us to follow. It is with this same understanding Paul says in 1 Corinthians 9:9, "For it is written in the law of Moses, Thou shalt not muzzle the ox when he treadeth out the corn." Do you suppose God's care is for the ox, or is not the verse written for our sakes? Surely for our sakes. As if the apostle had said: "God's care is not for the ox but for us." Not that God does not govern and provide for all creatures, but that he does not write and speak for them. What should he write and speak to oxen? Only to man does he speak. So here; although the words are about Christ, they are not directed to him but to us, for our learning: we, too, are to conduct ourselves as the Scriptures tell us Christ and his saints have done.

Mark the book the apostle here presents for the perusal and study of Christians—none other than the holy Scriptures. And he tells us it contains doctrine for us. Now if our doctrine is to be found in the Bible, we certainly should not seek it elsewhere; all Christians should make daily use of this book.

Observe, however, what the devil has accomplished through the Catholics. It was not enough for them to throw the Bible under the table, to make it so rare that few doctors of the holy Scriptures possess a copy, much less read it; but lest it be brought to public notice they have branded it with infamy. For they blasphemously say it is obscure; we must follow the interpretations of men and not the pure Scriptures. What else is their proceeding but giving Paul the lie here where he says the Bible is our manual of instruction? They say it is obscure and calculated to mislead.

How was God to reward such blasphemers and criminal destroyers of the Scriptures? Had he consulted with me about the matter, I would have entreated him—since they cast reproach upon his clear word, declaring it obscure and unsafe, and exclude it from the sight and knowledge of men, throwing it under the table—to give them in its stead Aristotle and Averrois, along with the endless statutes and fallacies of the Pope; to let them rave after these, studying Aristotle all the days of their lives and learning nothing; and yet to permit the dolts to be crowned masters of the liberal arts and doctors of the holy Scriptures.

Yet up to this time none of them have understood a single line in Aristotle, or at most have learned no more than a five-year-old child or the most depraved dolt knows. For Aristotle is a hundredfold more obscure than the holy Scriptures. If you would know what he teaches, I will tell you in few words: "A potter can make a pot from clay; a blacksmith cannot unless he learns how." If there is anything in Aristotle more exalted than this, believe not a word I have said. Demand of me to prove it and I will.

I say this to show how well Christ has rewarded the Catholics for denouncing his Scriptures as obscure and unsafe, and for perverting their design; for he permits the Catholics to read the writings of a dead heathen, who is not strong in real science, no, not in anything but darkness. What I have cited is the very best thing in Aristotle. I say nothing of his virulent and fatal positions. The universities deserve annihilation. Nothing more pernicious and satanic ever has been or ever will be on earth.

Now, let us return to Paul. He tells us here what we should read and where we should seek our doctrine. Were there any other book he would have designated it. Further, he shows the nature of the fruit resulting from perusal of the Bible; for he says, "That through patience and through comfort of the scriptures we might have hope." Now let all other doctrine present itself, let all other books be introduced, and see if they have any virtue or power to comfort a single soul in its least tribulation. Truly, no comfort but that of God's word is possible to the soul. But where will we find God's word except in the Scriptures? What do we accomplish by reading other books to the exclusion of the Book? Other books may have power to slay us, indeed, but no book except the holy Scriptures has power to comfort us. No other bears the title here given by Paul—book of comfort—one that can support the soul in all tribulations, helping it not to despair but to maintain hope. For thereby the soul apprehends God's word and, learning his gracious will, cleaves to it, continuing steadfast in life and death. He who knows not God's will must doubt, for he is unaware what relation he sustains to God.

But how shall I express the situation? The calamity is beyond the power of words, even inconceivable. The evil spirit has accomplished his design; he has suppressed the Book and introduced in its stead so many books of human doctrine that we may well say we are deluged with them. Yet these contain only error, falsehood, darkness, venom, death, destruction, hell and the devil. This condition of things our abominable ingratitude has merited.

Observe the aptness of Paul's expression where he links patience with the comfort of the Scriptures. The Bible does not remove adversity, suffering and death. No, it simply reveals the holy cross—Paul calls it the Word of the Cross—therefore patience is necessary. In the midst of suffering, however, the Bible consoles and strengthens, that our patience may not fail but press on unto victory. Under the strong comfort of God's solacing assurance that he is present to direct, the soul bears up with courage and joy beneath its sufferings.

This life is simply a mortification of the old Adam, which must die. So patience is essential. Again, since the life to come is not evident to mortal sense, it is necessary for the soul to have something to which it may cleave in patience, something to help it to a partial comprehension of that future life, and upon which it can rest. That something is God's

Word. To it the soul cleaves; therein it abides, and therein is conveyed from this earthly life to the life to come as in a safe ship. Thus does the hope of the soul continue steadfast.

Mark you, the real mission of the Scriptures is to comfort the suffering, distressed and dying. Then he who has had no experience of suffering or death cannot at all understand the comfort of the Bible. Not words but experience must be the medium of tasting and finding this comfort. Paul mentions "patience" before "comfort of the Scriptures" to indicate that he who, unwilling to endure suffering, seeks consolation elsewhere cannot taste the comfort of the Word. It is the province of the Word alone to comfort. It must therefore meet with patience first. It is jealous and will not permit human relief on a level with itself, which would be to frustrate the purpose of patience and suffering.

Now, it is no small cross and calls for no little measure of patience to bear the imperfections and sins of our neighbors. In some instances these things are oppressive enough to evoke, on the part of the sufferers, desire for death, either for themselves or someone else. To maintain Christian patience under these trials, the afflicted must comfort themselves with those portions of Scripture that show Christ's example. They will be helped to steadfastness and submission in suffering by perceiving that for their sakes Christ has submitted to far greater suffering, and has taken upon himself the infinitely heavier burden of their sins in the effort to redeem them.

Note, the comfort accompanying this patience is productive of a firm hope in Christ that we shall be like him. By contemplation of his record we are assured that for our sakes he has submitted, and continues to submit, to suffering. But to him who forgets Christ's example and the Scriptures, there remains very little comfort and patience, even when reason and material things have done their best to comfort him. For their efforts must be ineffectual. They cannot reach the inmost life of the heart. All the patience and comfort they are capable of affording is merely visionary.

"Now, the God of patience and consolation grant you to be like-minded one toward another according to Christ Jesus."

This epistle lesson should have commenced here. This verse has reference to the imperfections of both our faith and our conduct, but more especially to the frailties of faith, as we shall see. It is a prayer, with which Paul follows his preaching and teaching and concludes his letter to the Romans. Lest one might presume to exercise patience and to know the comfort of the Scriptures all by his own power, Paul in his prayer reminds us they are gifts of God, to be obtained through prayer. Particularly is it beyond our power to bear with the imperfections of others and to preserve the simple unity of faith.

Therefore, Paul says, "God of patience and of consolation;" that is, God is the Lord, and grants patience and consolation. Just as he is the God of heaven and earth, so is he the God of patience and consolation. All are his gifts and his creatures. Paul says God "grants" patience and comfort; we do not possess them of ourselves. If they are granted they are not of nature but of grace, and are gifts. If God does not direct his Word to the heart to fit the needs of the individual, the heart will never discover this patience and consolation. Indeed, where God does not grant them, the Scripture is neglected and human doctrine sought, as in the case of condemned Catholicism. But where he grants grace to search the Scriptures first, he gives likewise patience and consolation. There is no more marked manifestation of God's wrath than the fact that he permits the decline of his spoken and written Word; so not undesignedly the apostle uses the particular language of this prayer. On the other hand, God gives no greater blessing than when he exalts his Word among us and permits it to be read. Truly, then, we should all repeat this prayer with the apostle.

"To be like-minded one towards another." What do these words imply? How can the weak be "minded" like the strong? The phrase means each to tolerate the prejudices of another, and think that may be good which appears proper to another. Prejudice is the cause of all parties, sects, discord and heresy. As the proverb says, "Pleased with his own way is everyone, Hence the land with fools is overrun." Paul here would arrest self-pleasing and prejudice. Nothing is more intolerable and pernicious to the Christian faith and the Church than prejudice. The victim of it cannot rid himself of the fault. He must follow his own way, differing from the commonly-accepted one. He must establish a course pleasing to himself. This is the cause of the many parties and various customs in the different institutions and cloisters of the world, all mutually discordant. Each one is best pleased with his own choice and condemns the way of others.

But the apostle enjoins the Romans to be of one mind and tolerant of one another. The weak in conscience should accept as right what they of strong faith and sound conscience observe. The effort should be for a oneness of faith and conscience, and a sameness of opinion; and to avoid the wrangling occasioned by conflicting personal ideas of what is right. He would have them illustrate the psalmist's declarations (Ps. 68:6), "God setteth the solitary in families;" and (Ps. 133:1), "Behold, how good and how pleasant it is for brethren to dwell together in unity!" For instance, should one of weak faith observe one whose faith is strong eat meat or indulge in drink, or do what to him appears sinful, let him refrain from judging, even though he would not and could not do likewise. He should be of Paul's opinion on the subject: "Let each man be fully assured in his own mind" (Rom. 14:5). Then malice, contention and condemning may be avoided, and unanimity of purpose and disposition maintained. On the other hand, if the weak in faith is unable to do as his stronger brethren, they should not force him to it or despise him, but be content to tolerate him in regard to his eating, drinking and doing until he is likewise strong. Paul says, "Him that is weak in faith receive ye, yet not for decision of scruples" (Rom. 14:1). That is, ye shall not compel him saying, "This is right and that wrong," but treat him considerately and instruct him until he, too, shall become strong.

It is not necessary that we should all follow the same occupation. One may be a smith and another a tailor without impairing unity of faith and purpose, only let one tolerate the outward calling of the other. If some foolish individual were to interfere and teach that the occupation of a smith is an ungodly trade, he would be responsible for erring consciences and weakened faith. As privilege of occupation is right, so in the external things of meats, apparel and place, we are at liberty to follow our own pleasure. Then he who comes along and teaches it is wrong for you to use such and such things, as the Pope and the clergy teach, causes you to err. On the other hand, if another comes saying you must use certain things, he likewise causes you to err. But he who pursues a medium course, teaching liberty in the matter, not condemning you but permitting you to retain your own custom until you extricate yourself, and at the same time hard presses the wolves that would force you into that custom as a thing not optional but binding—this teacher gives you true instruction.

It is not wrong to fast in honor of the name of an apostle, or to confess during Lent. But neither does he who omits these things commit any evil by this omission. Let him who desires to fast and make confession, do so, but let not one censure, judge, condemn or quarrel with his fellow over the matter. One individual should be like-minded with another—tolerant of what the other does and regarding his action as right because in itself blameless.

He deserves censure who in these questions rashly presumes to judge according to the dictates of his own doctrine and destroys this unity saying, "Do so and you do right; do not so and you do wrong." He is an apostle of the devil, and his teaching is the doctrine of Satan. This is the manner of the Pope and the Catholics. It pertains not to shepherds but to wolves to preach doctrine of this character. Under such a condition of things, Christian unity must be dissolved. Difference of opinion becomes manifest: "You are a heretic"; "you are disobedient to the Church"; "you do wrong," and so on—just what the devil desires.

Having destroyed unity, taken captive the conscience and deprived of liberty, the Pope proceeds to take your money. Then he gives you a bill of exchange permitting you to eat butter, eggs, and meat, a privilege Christ gave you in the Gospel, a privilege whereof the Pope robbed you and which he as the pious shepherd sells to you again. But your indulgence in the privilege again, gives offense to your fellows. In short, the government of the Pope so abounds with grasping and re-grasping, with offense and repetition of offenses, with exchanges and re-exchanges, that it is plainly evident it simply belongs to the designing devil who effects confusion of conscience until no one is able to comprehend the right course.

But I refer to toleration only in the things wherein we are at liberty to be lenient. We should resist the Pope with his wicked and foolish laws as we would resist a wolf; and yet we are to permit the weak in faith to continue in their practices for a time, until we are able finally to extricate them from error. They must not be too hastily and rashly rejected, with disastrous results to their consciences.

But in things not optional with us, things prescribed or prohibited by Christ, there is little room for disputation, whether it be the weak in conscience or the strong who are concerned. In such case every individual, the least as well as the greatest, is under obligation to withstand the Pope; for instance, when he and all his followers teach that the mass is to be regarded as in the nature of a sacrifice and a good work. This is the most monstrous abomination that ever arose on earth. On it is founded the Pope's government with all its cloisters and other institutions. In this error no one is excusable, whether weak or strong; for Christ instituted the mass as a sacrament and testament. No one can sell or transfer it or give it away. As in the case of baptism, each must receive it for himself. There are in the Pope's canons many more abominations similar to this misuse of the mass. Indeed, considering the foundation, it is easy to perceive the character of the building. Everything existing in papal prerogatives is the wantonness of the devil, from turret to foundation. He who does not believe it, will experience it.

The apostle enjoins us to be like-minded "according to Christ Jesus"; that is, from a Christian point of view. For unbelievers, too, are like-minded, but according to the flesh, the world and the devil, and not according to Christ. The Jews were of one mind against God and his Christ, as Psalm 2:2 tells us. Christian unity resists sin and everything opposed to the religion of Christ without, however, committing or designing any sin. It works to the unifying of Christians generally, first with reference to faith and then to outward conduct.

When one is weak in faith and defective in conduct, the spirit of Christian unity, though deploring his condition, does not forsake him, much less disparage, reject or condemn him. His Christian fellow is interested in his welfare and conducts himself toward the weak one as he would himself be treated, and as Christ has indeed treated him in similar and more important matters. Thus is perpetuated that principle wherein the individual follows the way approved of others, conforming to their views and adhering to the same opinions. But the obstinate pursue a course quite the reverse, forsaking, rejecting and judging him who differs from them, and following their own ways, guided by their own opinions; as do the orders of Catholicism, and other sects.

"That with one accord ye may with one mouth glorify the God and Father of our Lord Jesus Christ."

All the good we can do to God is to praise and to thank him. This is the only true service we can render him, according to his words in Psalm 50:23, "Whoso offereth the sacrifice of thanksgiving glorifieth me; and to him that ordereth his way aright will I show the salvation of God." We receive all blessings from him, in return for which we should make the offering of praise. If anything else purporting to be service to God is presented for your consideration rest assured it is erroneous and delusive. For instance, the distracted world attempts to serve God by setting apart houses, churches, cloisters; vestures, gold-trimmed, silk and every other kind; silver vessels and images; bells and organs, candles and lamps; the money for which expense should have been appropriated to the poor if the object was to make an offering to God. Further, it keeps up a muttering and wailing in the churches day and night. But true praise and honor of God, a service that cannot be confined to place or person, is quietly ignored the world over. The pretenses of priests and monks about their system of exercises being service to the Lord, are false and delusive.

Service to God is praise of him. It must be free and voluntary, at table, in the chamber, cellar, garret, in house or field, in all places, with all persons, at all times. Whosoever teaches otherwise is no less guilty of falsehood than the Pope and the devil himself.

But how shall there be with us honor and praise of God, true service to him, when we neither love him nor receive his blessings? And how shall we love him when we do not know him and his blessings? And how shall we know him and his blessings when no word is preached concerning them and when the Gospel is left to lie under the table? Where the Gospel is not in evidence, knowledge of God is an impossibility. Then to love and praise him is likewise impossible. As a further consequence it is necessarily impossible for divine service to exist. Even if all the choristers were one chorister, all the priests one priest, all the monks one monk, all the churches one church, all the bells one bell; in brief if all the foolish services offered to God in the institutions, churches and cloisters were a hundred thousand times greater and more numerous than they are, what does God care for such carnivals and juggling?

Therefore, God complains most of the Jews in the second chapter of Micah, because they silenced his praise, while at the same time, they piped, blared and moaned like we do. True divine service of praise cannot be established with revenues, nor be circumscribed by laws and statutes. High and low festivals have nothing to do with it. It emanates from the Gospel, and certainly is as often rendered by a poor, rustic servant as by a great bishop.

It is plainly evident who have abolished divine service and still daily suppress it. They are none but that hopeless rabble, the Pope and his blockheads the bishops and priests, monks and nuns, whose great boast is of their divine services; who delight to be called the spiritual class and, by their juggling, grasp the advantages and honors of the world and live in riotousness. Yet they pretend to help others to heaven with their foolish works and no mention of the Gospel. Indeed, they persecute and condemn the Gospel, giving Peter just occasion to term them children of condemnation.

Note, Paul says divine service must be rendered with "one mind" and with "one mouth." We render divine service when we are harmonious, and when we recognize our common equality and our common blessings in Christ; when none exalts himself above another nor assumes special advantages.

Do you ask how it is we are equal, I reply: All outside of Christ are equally condemned. One needs Christ as much as another. When converted, all receive the same baptism and sacrament, the same faith, the same Christ and Spirit, the same Gospel—in a word, the same God. Here in this wilderness the heavenly bread is impartially distributed. Then how can it possibly be right for one to exalt himself over his fellow spiritually, one priest above the other? What can he have that surpasses Christ? And each has the same Christ, and Christ receives each one unreservedly.

True, one may embrace Christ more fervently than another; he may love him more and be more steadfast in his faith. Nevertheless, he has not for that received of Christ more than another. Christ is one and the same Christ to all, and in the things of salvation alike to everyone. Therefore he is truly Christ. Since there is one common blessing for the weak and the firm in faith, for the strong in Christian conduct and for the erring, one should not esteem another more lightly than himself, nor reject him. He is to recognize his fellow as an equal. Then shall praise to God arise harmoniously, and emanate as from one heart and one mouth. For so each individual praises God, and heart and mouth are actuated by the same impulse common to his fellows. All recognize Christ and render thanksgiving for what they receive through him; as prophesied in Psalm 72:15, "Men shall pray for him continually; they shall bless him all the day long." But he who offers thanks simply for his own advantages or possessions, destroys unanimity of purpose and expression, and belongs not to the communion of saints. Thus the Catholics and sects do. From them we never hear praise of Christ, but praise of their own works.

That Paul calls us to praise "the Father of our Lord Jesus Christ," and not to confine our praise to Christ, is worthy of special notice in our day when we extol the honor of the saints so highly that we trust in them and fail to press into God's very presence. We find one satisfied in calling upon St. Barbara and obtaining her favor, while there is no certain knowledge that she is a saint. Another is satisfied with Christofel, which is without doubt one of the greatest fictions and lies. But scarcely anyone is satisfied to honor the Virgin Mary and have her favor.

I fear abominable idolatry will thus gain ground, because we place in the saints the confidence and trust that should be placed in God alone, and expect from them what we can receive from God alone; and if no other evil were involved, it is a question whether the worship and honor of saints is supported by a passage or example in Scripture, and whether it is not contrary to this and like sayings of Paul, which teach us to press into the presence of God and place all our trust in him and expect everything we need for him. Christ, too, through the whole Gospel, points us to the Father. He came into the world that we should through him come to the Father.

To come to the Father does not mean to walk on bodily feet to Rome or to fly to heaven on wings. It means to rely upon God with sincere confidence as upon a gracious parent; as the opening of the Lord's Prayer implies. In proportion as we have such confidence of heart, do we come nearer to the Father. Both reason and experience must confess, if the heart trusts in God, the Creator, that all trust in creatures vanishes, whether in saints in heaven or upon earth. Therefore Peter says,

> "Knowing that ye were redeemed, not with corruptible things, with silver or gold, but with precious blood, as of a lamb without blemish and without spot, even the blood of Christ . . . so that your faith and hope might be in God" (1 Pet. 1:18-21).

And Paul says, "Through whom [Christ] also we have had our access by faith into this grace," etc. (Rom. 5:2).

I admit that some can make a proper use of honoring the saints and the virgin Mary; though it is seldom they do. The example is dangerous and it should not be introduced into the congregation as a practice. The teaching of Christ and of all the apostles is, that we should cheerfully approach God the Father alone through Christ. For it soon happens, because of man's terrible fall, that people seek comfort more from the saints than from God, and pray to their names for help rather than to God. It is a perverted, an unchristian, state of things that exists at present. I fear the world is full, yes, full, of idolatry.

God permits the worshiper of saints at times to receive help and perform wonders; yet, he does so through the agency of the devil. For it is God who gives to the servants of Satan their bodies and lives, their possessions and honor, and this he does through the agency of Satan. This is plainly evident; like a rich prince may give a treasure to one knave through another knave. Hence we are not to build upon miraculous signs nor upon the example of the multitude, but alone upon the teachings of Christ, or of his apostles, in this and all cases.

Now, while Christ is our common blessing, as before said, we should at the same time ascribe all to the Father; for Christ is the Father's gracious manifestation whereby our hearts are drawn to himself. So we should confidently love and praise the Father for his lavish blessings. With such exercise our hearts will learn to comfort themselves in him and to look to him for every blessing in life or death; but this through Christ and not through merit in ourselves. Christ was given that by him we might thus confidently approach the Father. John 14:6 declares, "No one cometh unto the Father, but by me."

Notwithstanding Christ is truly God and one might safely repose confidence in him, yet he constantly points to the Father; for he would not have mankind continue to trust in his humanity as the disciples did before his suffering, instead of lifting its thoughts above his humanity, up to his divinity. We must look upon Christ's humanity as enabling him to be a way, an evidence, a work of God, whereby we come to God. We are to place our whole confidence in God, and in him alone, being very careful not to devote any portion of it to the mother of God or any saint and so set up an idol in our hearts.

> **"Wherefore receive ye one another, even as Christ also received you, to the glory of God."**

What is the significance here of that word "wherefore?" "There are two reasons," the apostle would say to the Romans,

> "Why ye should receive one another. The first is, because of Christ's example. As ye have heard, the Scripture presents Christ to us as one upon whom fell the infamy of our sins—for us he was ignominious in God's sight—and who did not despise, reject or revile us, but received us that he might redeem us from our sins. We are, then, under particular obligation to receive one another."

The other reason the apostle presents for our receiving one another is that thus we contribute to the praise and honor of God. This we learn from Christ. He everywhere testifies that all he does is in obedience to his Father's will, and that he came for no other purpose than to do the will of God. It is certain, then, he bore the ignominy of our sins simply because it was his Father's will.

Mark the exceeding mercy of the Father's controlling will in placing upon his beloved and only Son our sins, and permitting him to bear the shame of them, merely that we might escape condemnation therefore. Now, a true recognition of this, God's gracious will, must evoke sincere love and praise to him and gratitude for his mercy. For, once the individual glimpses the Father's merciful will, he has a conscience so happy and serene he cannot restrain himself but must honor and praise God for his priceless blessings.

Note, Paul says Christ has in himself upheld the honor of God by receiving us and bearing, yes, exterminating, our sins. So should we likewise take upon ourselves the burdens, the sins and imperfections, of our neighbors, and bear with and help to reform them. When such Christian conduct is manifest before sinners and the spiritually weak, their hearts are attracted to God and forced to exclaim:

> "Truly, he must be a great and gracious God, a righteous Father, whose people these are; for he desires them not to judge, condemn nor reject us poor, sinful and imperfect ones, but rather to receive us, to give us

aid and to treat us as if our sins and imperfections were their own. Should we not love and exalt such a God? Should we not praise and honor him and give him the implicit confidence of our hearts in all things? What must be the character of that God who desires his people to be so noble?"

Mark you, this is the praise God would have from us, that we receive one another and regard our neighbor's condition as our own. Such conduct on our part would encourage others to believe and would strengthen the faith of believers. But where will we find in all the world any who follow Christ's example in this respect? Only tyrants, yes, devils, rule in church offices, who do nothing but excommunicate and condemn, drive and hound the people.

MISSIONS TO THE HEATHEN

"Now I say that Christ hath been made a minister of the circumcision for the truth of God, that he might confirm the promises given unto the fathers, and that the Gentiles might glorify God for his mercy."

THE APOSTLE HAS submitted to the Romans his sentiment that, in obedience to the example of Christ, they should receive one another, to the honor of God, and make no distinction between Christ's people, whether saints or sinners, strong or weak, rich or poor, since all are entitled to the same privileges. For all have the same blessings in Christ, who creates unity of heart, spirit, mind and word and renders common all things, whether spiritual or temporal, and however diverse they may be. Now Paul goes on to establish his position with strong passages of Scripture. Standing between Jews and gentiles as an arbitrator and mediator, he by the use of scriptural authority dissipates all causes of discord. He would say: "You Jews cannot reject the gentiles, even though they do not follow your customs in eating and drinking, for they have the very same Christ you have, according to Scripture prophecy." Again, "You gentiles cannot despise the Jews for not conforming to your ways in the matter of eating and drinking, for the Scripture promises to them the same Christ you profess."

"Now," Paul's argument is, "since the Scripture gives to all equal privileges in Christ, and Jews and gentiles are brought together under his authority, and since outside of Christ is naught for anyone, but in him everyone has all things—in view of these facts, why contend, why judge one another and stir up factions? Why not much rather receive one another in kindness as Christ received you? No one is favored over another and no one has less than another. Why then contend, and create schisms, over the question of meats, drink, clothing; over observance of time and place; over manners and such things? These are not vital in any respect; they are temporal things, outside of Christ, and contribute nothing to salvation. Let every man exercise the liberty he desires in these matters. If any is still weak in faith and has not freedom of conscience, patiently bear with him till he becomes strong, for your lenience will cost you nothing; you will still have Christ unreservedly."

To understand Paul's words here we must remember he is wont to refer to the Jewish people as "the circumcision." For they practiced the rite. Circumcision was a token whereby they were distinguished from other peoples. Such metaphors are often employed; for instance, we refer to women when we say, "Misfortune is oft woven with a weft of tresses"; to monks in the words, "Observe, what the cowl may not do"; or designate the priests when we exclaim, "How avaricious the bald pate!" And horsemen are indicated by the words "spurs" and "stirrups." It is in this metaphorical sense Paul, referring to a characteristic sign, terms the Jews "the circumcision" and the gentiles "præputium," "the uncircumcision": "They saw that I had been intrusted with the Gospel of the uncircumcision, [that is, of the uncircumcised gentiles] even as Peter with the Gospel of the circumcision [that is, of the Jews]" (Gal. 2:7-8). And again: "Remember, that once ye, the Gentiles in the flesh, who are called Uncircumcision by that which is called Circumcision," etc. (Eph. 2:11). So here he says, "I say that Christ hath been made a minister of the circumcision"; that is, of the Jewish people.

Using a convenient term, he calls Christ a "minister," as he calls all preachers and apostles ministers. "What then is Apollos? and what is Paul? Ministers through whom ye believed" (1 Cor. 3:5). The substance of the apostle's words is this: Jesus Christ was a minister of the circumcision. That is, a preacher, teacher, apostle, messenger, sent from God to the Jewish people. For Christ never preached to the gentiles. He was not sent to them, but to the Jews only.

But Christ was a minister to the Jews, not because of their merit, but as here stated, "for the truth of God." And what do we understand by those words? God promised Abraham, Isaac and Jacob that Christ should be born of their seed. To maintain God faithful in his promises, Christ came in fulfilment thereof. Thus is the truth of God proven; God keeps his promises. For the sake of God's truth, or in other words, that God might be proven truthful, and not for the sake of merit on the part of anyone, Christ became an apostle and a minister of the circumcision. This explanation is necessary to satisfy the succeeding phrase, "that he might confirm the promises given unto the fathers." Observe the apostle's meaning in the words "the truth of God"—the fulfilment and establishment of the divine promise made to the patriarchs concerning Christ.

True, Jews and gentiles have Christ in common, yet the promise was not to the gentiles; it was to the Jews exclusively. Paul tells us in Romans 3:2 that the Jews "were intrusted with the oracles of God"; and again, in Romans 9:4, that the Law was given to them. So, too, Christ came to the Jews alone, as he says himself: "I was not sent but unto the lost sheep of the house of Israel" (Matt. 15:24). It was the peculiar privilege of the Jews to have Christ promised to them, and to be able to await his coming. But to the gentiles was nothing promised, and they awaited nothing. At the same time, Jews and gentiles are on common ground in the fact that, Christ being promised of pure grace, he was given to the gentiles also. After the promise was made to the Jews, the gentiles had just reason to regard the coming Messiah as given to them also.

The Jews, then, have Christ not only through grace in the promise, but also because of the truth of God in fulfilment of his promise. But the gentiles have neither the grace of the promise nor the truth of fulfilment. They have merely the naked, unpromised, unexpected mercy

Christ gives to them. There is no promise, and no obligation for fulfilment of the truth of God. Yet, the Scriptures having revealed that the gentiles should obtain Christ, though without promise, hope or expectation, the Scriptures must be fulfilled. Therefore, one people is not favored over the other. But Christ was given to the Jews through divine promise and divine truth, and to the gentiles through pure, unexpected mercy.

Since the Scriptures contain a promise to the Jews and a prediction concerning the gentiles, the two peoples have a common bond in Christ. Hence each should receive the other as a participant in the common blessing. The Jews are not to despise the gentiles; because the Scriptures say the gentiles shall praise God for his mercy, and how shall the Jews despise those who enjoy God's mercy and praise him for it? On the other hand, the gentiles should not despise the Jews; for to the latter was Christ promised, and in fulfilment of the promise he became their minister and preacher, making God faithful to his word.

Let us see what is Paul's intent in declaring: "I say that Christ hath been made a minister of the circumcision for the truth of God, that he might confirm the promises given unto the fathers." Why this claim? Doubtless that none may despise the Jews, but rather receive them, in obedience to the example of Christ. Christ did not despise them; nay, he was even publicly promised and given to them as their own minister, preacher and apostle. But what do you say, Paul, in regard to the gentiles?

> "I do not say they are promised aught, but I say they enjoy and praise the mercy of God given them without promise, as the Scriptures imply. So, too, none should despise the gentiles, but rather receive them, in obedience to Christ's example."

As Christ is a common bond between Jews and gentiles, though not given to each people in just the same way; so should there be unity among us. We must receive one another, bear one another's burdens and have patience with imperfections, regardless of personal appearance, name, condition or anything else.

> "Therefore I will give praise unto thee among the Gentiles, and sing unto thy name."

Now the apostle goes on to quote some Scripture passages revealing the fact that the gentiles shall praise God for his mercy. This first quotation is found in Psalm 18:49, and also in Psalm 108:3. The words are spoken by the prophet for Christ, as in both cases the whole Psalm makes plain. Now, if this declaration is to be verified, Christ must be present with the gentiles, not physically but spiritually. For unless Christ is present spiritually, praise of him is not forthcoming; but the singing of his praise is guarantee of his spiritual presence. So this quotation forces us to conclude that the gentiles shall believe in Christ and possess him; in other words, enjoy the mercy of God. Yet the verse makes no promise to them. It is merely a revelation concerning their future conduct.

We have before mentioned what constitutes true service of God. Here the prophet refers to it as praising and singing unto God's name. And so is it defined throughout the Scriptures. Now, praise is simply a confession of blessings received. The Hebrew and apostolic word in this verse is "confitebor," "I will confess thee"; meaning, "I will thank and praise thee and declare, All have I received from thee."

> "And again he saith, Rejoice, ye Gentiles, with his people."

These words are quoted from Deuteronomy 32:43, where Moses says, "Rejoice, O ye nations, with his people." The Hebrew, however, admits of the rendering, "Rejoice, ye Gentiles, with him" (understand "his people"). It is with this thought of God, it seems to me, the apostle introduces the quotation. Yet, whether we read it thus or otherwise, clearly no one praises the people of God, nor rejoices with him, unless he be partaker of God's blessings and own him God. For he who does not possess God and his blessings is an enemy to God's people, cursing and persecuting them, as God says in Genesis 12:3, "I will bless them that bless thee, and him that curseth thee will I curse." Here you see, they who bless God's people are partakers of his blessings. So this second quotation teaches conclusively that the gentiles shall become Christians.

> **"And again, Praise the Lord, all ye Gentiles; and let all the peoples praise him."**

This verse is Psalm 117:1-2. It also has reference to true service of God. Therefore it, too, teaches that the gentiles shall be the people of God. For only they serve (praise and honor) God who are his people.

> **"And again, Isaiah saith, There shall be the root of Jesse, and he that ariseth to rule over Gentiles, on him shall the Gentiles hope."**

We have this declaration in Isaiah 11:10. In Hebrew it reads, "And it shall come to pass in that day that the root of Jesse, that standeth for an ensign of the people, unto him shall the nations seek; and his resting-place shall be glorious." The meaning evidently is that the gentiles shall possess Christ and he shall reign over them. Paul makes a slight change in the words, following the rendering of the old translators who wrote the Bible in the Greek language. The meaning of the quotation is the same, however. The "root" of Jesse should not be understood here as "stem" or "tree" in the genealogical sense, as the artist would delineate the "tree" of Jesse, the father of David, with its many branches; and as we understand when we sing of the blessed Virgin, "the stem of Jesse has sprung forth." That would be altogether a forced construction. Christ himself, and none other, is the "stem" or "root." The construction of this passage from Isaiah makes that meaning plain, for it says practically, "The gentiles shall hope for the stem or root of Jesse, which is to rule the nations," etc. This prophecy cannot be made to refer to the human Jesse or to our blessed Virgin.

Christ is the root of Jesse. He descended from the lineage of Jesse, through David, but in him physical descent ceased. He suffered and was buried in the grave as an ill-favored root, concealed from the world, and out of him grew that beautiful tree, the Christian Church, spreading out into all the world. The root of Jesse is properly delineated when portrayal includes the sufferings of Christ and their fruits.

Paul's assertion "and he that ariseth to rule over the Gentiles" is equivalent to the Hebrew "that standeth for an ensign of the people." It shows Christ's government a spiritual one. The Gospel raises him as a standard before the whole world, an ensign to which we must be loyal through faith. We do not see him physically; we behold him only through the ensign, the Gospel. And it is through the Gospel he reigns over men; not in a physical presence.

Again, the expression "on him shall the Gentiles hope" does not materially differ from the Hebrew rendering "to it shall the Gentiles seek." The meaning is, the gentiles shall look unto the root of Jesse and cleave only to him, placing all confidence and hope in him and finding in him their consolation. They shall seek for and desire naught else.

But the phrase "and his grave [resting-place] shall be glorious," contained in the quotation from Isaiah but omitted by the apostle, is not well rendered by Jerome, who thinks Isaiah refers to the glorious grave of Christ. Isaiah's thought was of Christ's rest being glorious; that is, his death should mean something more than that of ordinary mortals, to whom death is the end of glory. The glory of the root of Jesse had its beginning in his death. For not until then was he raised to true life and power, to real glory and honor—an ensign for the gentiles, and ruler of them. Indeed, then he was seated at the right hand of God, Lord over all things.

"Now the God of hope fill you with all joy and peace in believing, that ye may abound in hope, in the power of the Holy Spirit."

Paul concludes this passage with a noble prayer, desiring the Romans to be filled with joy and peace. He calls upon the "God of hope," referring to the hope God alone gives through Christ and in Christ.

The way we possess peace and joy we have before spoken of; the secret is in perceiving the will of God, how he gave Christ to bear our sins, which we are under obligation to believe. The more clearly we perceive his will, the stronger will be our faith, our hope and love.

Hence we must continually preach the Gospel—receive it and meditate upon it. For faith comes through no other medium than the Gospel.

The apostle says, in effect:

> "May God, who through the Gospel effects hope, grant you grace, enabling you to appropriate the Gospel and believe. Through believing, you first perceive Christ. Thereupon follow perfect peace and an assured conscience. These are blessings common to all, and you will have harmony among yourselves."

The Christian's peace and joy is something received, not as the gift of the world is received, through mortal sense, but through faith. He who is the source of your good, and from whom you derive your peace and joy, is not recognized by sight or touch. However, in the world you will have disquietude and grief. But learn that Christ is the common blessing of all and you will enjoy blessed peace. For all being alike rich, no one can begrudge another anything. This is what it means to have peace and joy through faith or in faith.

"That ye may abound in hope," continues the prayer. In other words, "that your hope may ever increase." Now, suffering and persecution contribute to the increase of hope. We are not given increased hope to decrease adversity; no, adversity is increased that hope may not rely on human power, but be established through the power of the Holy Spirit. For the Holy Spirit aids us, fortifying our hope and enabling us not to fear nor to flee from the disasters of the world; but to stand firm even unto death, and to overcome all evil; so that evil must flee from us and cease its attacks. Remember, it is hope in the power of the Holy Spirit, not in human weakness, that must do all this through the medium of the Gospel. As before said, "Through patience and through comfort of the Scriptures we have hope." Where the Gospel is not, there is neither hope, comfort, peace, joy, faith, love, Christ, God, nor anything good. Evidence of this fact is before us in the wretched, spiritless, carnal clerical orders, notwithstanding their much praying and holding of masses. From these things, O thou God of hope, of patience and of comfort, graciously preserve us. Amen.

3
Third Sunday in Advent

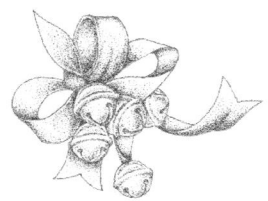

"Let a man so account of us, as of ministers of Christ, and stewards of the mysteries of God. Here, moreover, it is required in stewards, that a man be found faithful. But with me it is a very small thing that I should be judged of you, or of man's judgment; yea, I judge not mine own self. For I know nothing against myself; yet am I not hereby justified: but he that judgeth me is the Lord. Wherefore judge nothing before the time, until the Lord come, who will both bring to light the hidden things of darkness, and make manifest the counsels of the hearts; and then shall each man have his praise from God" (1 Corinthians 4:1-5).

STEWARDS OF THE MYSTERIES OF GOD

THIS EPISTLE SELECTION illustrates the Gospel lesson for the first Sunday in Advent, wherein we learned the disciples did not themselves ride on the colt, but led it to Christ and set him thereon. That is what the apostle does here. The Corinthians had come to divisions among themselves and to boasting of certain apostles as their leaders. With one party it was Peter, with another Paul, and with yet another Apollos. Each one exalted the apostle by whom he was baptized or was taught, or the one he regarded most eminent. Now comes Paul and interposes, permitting no one to boast of any apostle, and teaching them to laud Christ alone. He tells them it matters not by whom they were baptized and taught, but it is of the utmost importance that they all hold to Christ together and own allegiance to him alone. Paul beautifully teaches how the apostles are to be regarded.

The whole passage is a fierce thrust at Catholicism and the clerical government, as we shall see.

"Let a man so account of us, as of the ministers of Christ, and stewards of the mysteries of God."

The reference is to all apostles and all heirs to the apostolic chair, whether Peter, Paul, or any other. Let us, then, be very careful how we regard the apostles and bishops; we must attach neither too much nor yet too little importance to them. Not without reason did Paul—the Holy Spirit, in fact—make this restriction; and without doubt we are under obligation to follow it. The same limit here made concerning apostles applies to bishops. It designates the character of their office and the extent of their power. So when we see a bishop assuming more than this text gives him warrant for, we may safely regard him as a wolf, and an apostle of the devil, and avoid him as such. Unquestionably he must be Antichrist who in ecclesiastical government exceeds the authority here prescribed.

First, Paul warns us against receiving apostles or bishops as anything but "ministers of Christ;" nor should they desire to be regarded otherwise. But the term "minister of Christ" must not in this connection be understood as one who serves God, in the present acceptation of the phrase—praying, fasting, attendance upon Church services, and all the things styled "divine service" by ecclesiastical rites, institutions and cloisters, and by the whole clerical order. Theirs are merely humanly devised works and words, whereby Paul's teaching here and elsewhere is wholly obscured, even to the extent of making it impossible to know what he means by the "ministry of Christ." He has reference to the ministry that is an office. All Christians serve God but all are not in office. In Romans 11:13, also, he terms his office a ministry: "Inasmuch as I am an apostle of Gentiles, I glorify my ministry." And in the epistle selection preceding this (Rom. 15:8) he says, "I say that Christ hath been made a minister of the circumcision." Again (2 Cor. 3:6), "Who also made us sufficient as ministers of a new covenant; not of the letter, but of the spirit."

What language is forcible enough to serve me in the attempt to eradicate from the hearts of all Christians that error so deeply impressed of Catholicism wherein they interpret the ministry of Christ—or the service of God—in no other light than as their own works, performed to Christ without any authority to do them? Mark you, beloved, to serve Christ, or to serve God, is defined by Paul himself as to fulfil a Christ-ordained office, the office of preaching. This office is a service or ministry proceeding from Christ to us, and not from us to Christ. Note this carefully; it is important. Otherwise you cannot understand the design of the Pauline words, "ministry, ministration, to minister." So he always has it. Seldom does he speak of the service or ministry rendered primarily above them to God; it is usually of the ministry beneath them, to men. Christ, too, in the Gospel bids the apostles to be submissive and servants of others (Luke 22:26).

To make himself clearly understood in this matter of service, or ministry, Paul carefully adds to the word "ministers" the explanatory one "stewards," which can be understood in no other way than as referring to the office of the ministry.

He terms his office "service or ministry of Christ" and himself "minister of Christ," because he was ordained of God to the office of preaching. So all apostles and bishops are ministers of Christ; that is preachers, messengers, officers of Christ, sent to the people with his message. The meaning of the verse, then, is: Let every individual take heed not to institute another leader, to set up another Lord, to constitute another Christ. Rather be unanimously loyal to the one and only Christ. For we apostles are not your lords, nor your masters; we are not your leaders. We do not preach our own interests, nor teach our own doctrines. We do not seek to have you obey us, or give us allegiance and accept our doctrine. No, indeed. We are messengers and ministers of him who is your Master, your Lord and Leader. We preach his Word, enlist men to follow his commandments, and lead only into obedience. And in this light should you regard us, expecting of us nothing else than to bring the message. Though we are other persons than Christ, yet you do not receive through us another doctrine than his; another word, another government, nor another authority than his. He who so receives and regards us, holds the right attitude toward us, and receives, not us, but Christ, whom alone we preach. But he who does not so regard us, does us injustice, discards Christ, the one true Leader, sets up another in his stead and makes gods of us.

In Judges 8:22-23 we read that the children of Israel said to Gideon: "Rule thou over us, both thou, and thy son, and thy son's son also," to which Gideon answered, "I will not rule over you, neither shall my son rule over you: Jehovah shall rule over you." And in 1 Samuel 8:7 we are told that when the children of Israel desired a king of Samuel, God said, "They have not rejected thee, but they have rejected me, that I should not be king over them." Thus we see God cannot permit any authority to usurp his own among his people.

But perhaps you ask: "Where was the sin of the people when they desired Gideon to rule over them? Had not God given Gideon leadership in the contest, and did he not later provide many holy kings expressly for them?" I reply it was not a sin for the children of Israel to have sovereigns; it was not contrary to God's will; for there must be temporal authorities. But the sin consisted in the fact that, not content with God's government, they chose human government instead. Gideon and the holy kings did not extend their authority as rulers a hair's breadth farther than God's command warranted, and they did not regard themselves in any other light than as the servants or ministers of God; that is, they ruled according to God's direction and not according to their own. Thus was perpetuated God's government in its purity, and they were servants in it; as were the apostles servants in the word of Christ. Hence David sings of his own kingdom as identical with God's. He says,

> "Arise, O Jehovah, in thine anger: lift up thyself against the rage of mine adversaries, and awake for me; thou hast commanded judgment. And let the congregation of the peoples compass thee about; and over them return thou on high. Jehovah ministereth judgment to the peoples" (Ps. 7:6-8).

But where more authority is assumed than God's command gives, and where the magistrate attempts to rule according to human doctrines, or the subjects seek such leadership, idolatry results and the leader assumes a new character. The magistrate is no longer a servant or minister, but rules arbitrarily, without command of God. God says of them as he said to Samuel concerning the children of Israel: "They have not rejected the magistrate, but they have rejected me, that I should not reign over them." I refer here to spiritual matters, to the sovereignty of the soul, which must stand before God. Civil government is a matter that does not pertain to nor concern the soul.

Where divine leadership is shared with any other than God or Christ, there must also be doctrine and commandments differing from the doctrine and command of Christ. Service of Christ must immediately fail; Christ must be rejected for the establishment of a new sovereignty. Plainly enough, no one can be servant of Christ and at the same time teacher of his own message. The two conditions cannot exist at the same time. How can one be a servant of Christ if he does not teach Christ's message? Or how can he teach his own message when he is under obligation to teach only Christ's? If he advocates his own counsels, he makes himself lord and does not serve Christ. If he advocates Christ's counsels, he cannot himself be lord.

From this you may judge for yourself whence arises Catholicism and its ecclesiastical authority, with all its priests, monks and high schools. If these can prove they teach nothing but the message of Christ, we must regard them as his ministers or servants. But if we can prove they do not so teach, we must regard them as not his servants. Now it certainly is clear that their teaching is not the doctrine of Christ, but their own doctrine. Hence it is evident they constitute the kingdom of Antichrist and are servants of the devil. For Paul makes a firm stand here and declares: "Let a man so account of us as of the ministers of Christ."

Their claim that in addition to the teachings of Christ, the commandments of the Church may be taught—and they intimate that their teachings are the doctrines of the Church—is of no significance. Paul's teaching here continues to stand, that the Church belongs neither to Peter nor Paul, but to Christ only, and acknowledges none but the servants or ministers of Christ. You see, then, the blasphemy of the

Pope in crying obedience to his doctrines as the road to salvation, and disobedience to them, the road to damnation. Paul here makes obedience to these things a work of the devil; as he does also in 1 Timothy 4:1-3,

> "But the Spirit saith expressly, that in later times some shall fall away from the faith, giving heed to seducing spirits and doctrines of demons, through the hypocrisy of men that speak lies, branded in their own conscience as with a hot iron; forbidding to marry, and commanding to abstain from meats, which God created to be received with thanksgiving by them that believe and know the truth."

And Christ says: "My sheep hear my voice, and a stranger will they not follow, but will flee from him; for they know not the voice of strangers. I know mine own, and mine own know me" (John 10:5-14).

Note the harmony between Paul's teaching and this statement of Christ's that any other than the voice of Christ is a strange voice, the doctrine of the devil, and to be avoided. You see here Christ's own verdict in regard to doctrines, what his Church hears and teaches, and what are and what are not the commandments of the Church. The Church has no other doctrine than that of Christ, and no other obedience than to obey him. All the Catholics say, then, concerning obedience to the commandments of the Church is in the same class with what Paul calls speaking lies in hypocrisy, moved by false spirits and doctrines of devils.

The same is the meaning of the phrase "stewards of the mysteries of God." The word "steward" here signifies one who has charge of his lord's domestics; one whose office is the same as that of stewards in monasteries at the present day, or provosts in nunneries, or governors, managers and overseers of the sort. For "oekonomus" is Greek and signifies in English a "steward," or one capable of providing for a house and ruling the domestics. Christ in Matthew 24:45 calls such a one simply a servant: "Who then is the faithful and wise servant, whom his lord hath set over his household, to give them their food in due season?" Such a servant was Eliezer, the steward of Abram's house (Gen. 15).

Now, God's household is the Christian Church—ourselves. It includes pastors and bishops, overseers and stewards, whose office is to have charge of the household, to provide nourishment for it and to direct its members, but in a spiritual sense. Paul puts a distinction between the stewards of God and temporal stewards. The latter provide material nourishment, and exercise control of the physical person; but the former provide spiritual food and exercise control over souls. Paul calls the spiritual food "mysteries." The practice of providing it has so long been discontinued we do not now know what a steward is nor what is meant by "mysteries." Church officials imagine that when they baptize, celebrate mass and administer other sacraments, they exercise the mysteries, and that now there is no proper mystery but the mass. At the same time they know not the meaning of the term in this connection.

I cannot just now find a word in German equivalent to "mysterion," and it will be well to retain the Greek form, as we have with many other words. It is equivalent to "secret," something hidden from our eyes, invisible to all, and generally pertaining to words. For instance, a saying not easily understood is said to contain a hidden meaning, a secret, a "mysterion"—something is concealed therein. The concealment itself may properly be termed "mystery"; I call it a secret.

What, then, constitutes the mysteries of God? Simply Christ himself; that is, faith and the Gospel concerning Christ. The whole Gospel teaching is far beyond the grasp of our reason and our physical sense; it is hidden to the world. It can be apprehended only by faith; as Christ says in Matthew 11:25, "I thank thee, O father, Lord of heaven and earth, that thou didst hide these things from the wise and understanding, and didst reveal them unto babes." And as Paul tells us (1 Cor. 2:7-8), "We speak God's wisdom in a mystery, which none of the rulers of this world hath known."

Expressed in the clearest manner possible, "mystery" is the reception of the things of faith—that Christ the Son of God was born of a virgin, died and rose again, and all this that our sins might be forgiven. These things eye sees not nor reason comprehends. Indeed, as Paul says (1 Cor. 1:23), they are mere foolishness to the wise, and simply an offense to the self-righteous saints.

How can the natural man perceive, or reason acknowledge, that the man Christ is our life and salvation, our peace, our righteousness and redemption, our strength and wisdom, Lord of all creatures—that he is even God—and everything else the Scriptures testify of him? None can apprehend these truths except he hears and believes them through the Gospel. They are too far beyond sense and reason to be grasped by the natural man.

So, then, the mysteries of God are simply the blessings in Christ as preached through the Gospel and apprehended and retained by faith alone. Paul says relative to the matter, speaking on how men should behave themselves in the house of God: "Without controversy great is the mystery of godliness; he who was manifested in the flesh, justified in the spirit, seen of angels, preached among the nations, believed on in the world, received up in glory" (1 Tim. 3:16). This is spoken of Christ, who was manifest in the flesh. He dwelt among men who had flesh and blood like himself, yet he was still a mystery. That he was Christ, the Son of God, the life, the way, the truth and all good, was hidden.

Yet he was "justified in the Spirit;" that is, through the Spirit's influence believers received, acknowledged and retained him as all we have mentioned. "To justify" means simply to pronounce just, or at least to admit as just; as we have in Luke 7:29, "All the people when they heard, and the publicans, justified God." Again, in Psalm 51:4, "That thou mayest be justified when thou speakest." This is equivalent to saying: The believer in Christ justifies him, and acknowledges the truth that Christ alone is our life and righteousness and wisdom, and that we are sinners, condemned and perishing. For such Christ is, and such is his claim. He who acknowledges this his claim justifies him in the Spirit; but he who does not justify him relies upon his own works; he does not see himself condemned but contends against and condemns Christ. (This justification of Christ is effected by no one unless he possesses the Holy

Spirit, whose work alone it is. Flesh and blood cannot do it, even if it be publicly presented to our eyes and preached into our ears.)

The statement in Romans 1:4, "Christ was declared to be the Son of God with power, according to the spirit of holiness," has reference to justification. As if to say, "In unbelievers Christ is nothing; not only despised, but utterly condemned. But the saints whose life is in the Spirit who sanctifies them, strongly and boastfully maintain that he is the Son of God. To them it is proved and firmly settled."

Paul might have said, "We are the stewards of the wisdom of God, or of the righteousness of God," and so on. For all this Christ is; as he says (1 Cor. 1:30), "Who was made unto us wisdom from God, and righteousness and sanctification, and redemption." But this would have been specifying, and he desired to embrace in one word all the blessings in Christ which the preaching of the Gospel brings; so he styles them "mysteries." We may understand it as if he said, "We are spiritual stewards whose duty it is to minister the grace of God, the truth of God—but who can enumerate all? Let us briefly sum them up and say, the mysteries of God; mysteries and hidden things because faith alone can attain them."

He adopts the same style in Romans 1:4 when he comprises in one word how Christ was manifest in the flesh, justified in the Spirit, preached to the gentiles, and so on. Similarly, in 1 Timothy 3:16 he expresses it briefly in Greek, "oristheis," *determined.* In short, Christ was declared and determined, was received and regarded, as the Son of God, by angels, gentiles, the world, heaven and all things; since for this purpose he was manifested, justified, revealed, preached, believed, received, and so on. Hence he indicates it here by the plural word "mysteries," and in 1 Timothy 3:16 by the singular "mystery." The words are, however, equivalent in this connection. Christ is all in all, one mystery, and many mysteries, as expressed in the many mysterious blessings we have from him.

It is worthy of note that Paul adds to "mysteries" the modifier "of God;" he means the hidden things God grants and which exist in him. For the devil also has his mysteries, as Revelation 17:5 says, "Upon her forehead a name written, Mystery, Babylon the Great," etc. And again, in the seventh verse, "I will tell thee the mystery of the woman." The things over which the Pope and his priests now preside as stewards are mysteries of the latter class; for they intimate that their doctrine and deeds win heaven, when in reality they but conceal death and hell for all who trust therein. But the mysteries of God enfold life and salvation.

Thus we arrive at the apostle's meaning in the assertion that a minister of Christ is a steward in the mysteries of God. He should regard himself and insist that others regard him as one who administers to the household of God nothing but Christ and the things of Christ. In other words, he should preach the pure Gospel, the true faith, that Christ alone is our life, our way, our wisdom, power, glory, salvation; and that all we can accomplish of ourselves is but death, error, foolishness, weakness, shame and condemnation. Whosoever preaches otherwise should be regarded by none as a servant of Christ or a steward of the divine treasurer; he should be avoided as a messenger of the devil. So it follows:

FAITHFULNESS IN STEWARDS.

"Moreover, it is required in stewards, that a man be found faithful."

UPON THIS ALL depends. After faithfulness God inquires. Angels, men and all creatures look for and demand it; not the mere name or honor of steward will answer. The question is not whether one's bishopric be large or small; nor is it particularly important whether or no he be outwardly pious. The question is, does he faithfully execute the duties of his office, acting as a steward in the blessings of God? Paul here permits us much liberty to judge the doctrines and lives of our bishops, cardinals and all Catholics. The same faithfulness is also required by Christ: "Who then is the faithful and wise servant, whom his lord hath set over his household, to give them their food in due season?" (Matt. 24:45).

What is the nature of the faithfulness of the Catholics—how does it measure up? Tell me, who would be reformed or profited were any one bishop to have prominence and power enough to possess every bishopric, as the Pope tries to do? Who would be benefited if a bishop were so holy that his shadow would raise the dead? Who would be the gainer if he had wisdom equal to all the apostles and prophets? But none of these things are inquired after; the question is, Is he a faithful bishop? does he administer to the household of faith the Word of God? does he preach the Gospel and dispense the mysteries of God? Emphatically the inquiry is made upon these points. Here is where the individual is benefited. Above all things, then, faithfulness is demanded of stewards.

Now, measure the Pope and all the ecclesiasts by the requirements of this text. Tell me, what is the Pope seeking? Is not the sole purpose of all his grasping and raging to enable him to rule supremely and arbitrarily? His whole concern is for fame, power, position and wealth, for authority over all men. Through the Pope's blasphemous lips the devil deceitfully endeavors to emphasize the importance of obedience to popish laws, and the danger to the soul's salvation from disobedience. The Pope is not concerned about faithfulness to the Christian household. For tell me where in all his innumerable laws and commands—a veritable flood of them—where in the whole extent of his government, did you ever learn of his touching with a single word upon the mysteries of God? Or where has he preached the Gospel? All his utterances relate to quarrels, to prebends, or at best to the matter of pates and apparel. Indeed, he openly condemns the Gospel and the mysteries of God. And the bishops and ecclesiasts follow him with their endowments, cloisters and high schools.

They have so perverted apostolic faithfulness that with them a faithful bishop, abbot or ecclesiastical prelate is one who loyally manages, guards, improves and increases their temporal possessions—the heritage of St. Peter, the Castle of St. Moretz, the land of the holy cross, the interests of the Virgin and other concerns of the Church, in a word, their own emolument—under the name of God and of the saints; the world, even in its most sordid state, bears no comparison to them. Such are the princes, the bishops and prelates who have the credit of having governed well the Church; it matters not whether or no they have, during their whole lives, read or heard the Gospel, not to mention their disregard for their duty to preach it. The blasphemous tongue of the Pope, in its world-wide unrestraint, calls them good stewards of the blessings of God who are utterly useless, unless it be to fill the place of treasurer, assessor, guardian, bailiff, architect, mayor, plowman, butler or kitchen steward for some temporal lord. Such is their apostolic fidelity; this and nothing more.

In the meantime, souls are perishing. Divine interests are going to ruin. The wolf reigns and devours. In spiritual affairs the popish stewards see no danger and afford no security. They sit unconcernedly counting over their profits, attending to the interests of St. Laurence and with extreme faithfulness providing for the property of the Church—a faithfulness in return for which they are certain Christ has prepared for them no inferior seat in heaven. O wretched, lost, blinded multitude, how securely you are going on toward hell!

I cannot pass without notice here—for I must relate it as a warning against similar attempts—a trick of the devil which, I heard it said, he exhibited in time past at Merseburg, in our own country. It had to do with the golden cup of Emperor Henry. The Pope's beloved people zealously relate a certain falsehood, for which they obtain indulgences. They assert that the roasted Laurence, by casting the golden cup into the balance, got so much the better of the devil that he was forced to release the soul of the Emperor, in consequence of which he (the devil) was enraged to the extent of breaking an ear off the cup. Such gross, foolish, idle falsehoods are intended to blind us Christians from perceiving the devil's trickery. What is the devil's purpose in this fabrication? The whole thing is a design to establish by the miraculous, the wealth, luxury and delicate faithfulness of the prelates of which we have spoken. Thereby the weak-minded are to be induced to believe they can overcome the devil by presenting gifts to the Church. But Peter says this conquest is only to be effected by the power of faith. These are the signs Christ and Paul predicted would accompany the misleading of the elect from the faith.

A fidelity even more beautiful to contemplate exists among unspiritual lords and faithful stewards of the same class actively engaged in directing the spiritual welfare of souls. Certainly these are true stewards and the right sort! So extremely holy are they, St. Peter will have to be on his guard if he holds his place with them. They are our spiritual fathers—priests, monks and nuns—who exercise themselves in obedience to the Pope, the holy Church and every form of human institutions and orders and statutes. Among them are the paragon, the quintessence, the kernel, the marrow, the foundation—and how shall I enumerate all the honorable titles which they assume and hold from custom? Yes, far enough from custom! The beautiful little cat has pretty, smooth fur.

Here is where we find our good stewards and our unheard-of fidelity. How tenaciously, how rigorously and earnestly, they adhere to that sort of obedience and maintain those traditions. Yes, indeed, they are the proper saints. Few bishops who rigidly observe the holy, spiritual law can rank with them. But when we investigate their cloisters and review their doctrines and conduct, we find that no people on earth are less acquainted with the mysteries of God and farther from Christ. Indeed, they act as if mad, maliciously storming Christ with their own inventions. They are the Gog and Magog of the Revelation of John, contending against the Lamb of God. For they exalt their own works to the extermination of faith, and are termed the faithful stewards of God, as the wolf among the sheep is the shepherd.

Now, he that hath ears, let him hear what Paul says, "It is required in stewards, that a man be found faithful"; but he is faithful who is occupied with the mysteries of God. The conclusion, then, is: the Pope, the bishops, monks and nuns, the founders and inmates of universities, and all who with them build upon anything or are occupied with anything but Christ, the Gospel and true faith, though they may have indeed the name of servants and stewards of Christ, are in reality servants and stewards of the devil, their lord, and are engaged with his mysteries or secrets. Christ, in the saying we have quoted from Matthew, tells us further, the servant of the household should be not only faithful, but also wise, able to discern between the mysteries of God and the mysteries of the devil, that he may safely guard and keep himself and those committed to his care. For, as Paul says in 2 Corinthians 11:13-14, false apostles sometimes fashion themselves into true apostles of Christ, even as the devil transforms himself into an angel of light.

Where wisdom to discern the mysteries of God is lacking, the greater the faithfulness the greater the danger; as we perceive in the two mentioned cases of false, seductive faithfulness on the part of the unspiritual saints. Paul well knew how the mysteries of the devil would prevail; so, while silent in regard to every other qualification necessary for stewards, he points out faithfulness. Had our bishops remained faithful stewards of God, Catholicism and its peculiar spiritual orders undoubtedly would not have been introduced; the common spiritual order and life of faith would have been maintained. And were they now to return to faithfulness the strange special orders would soon pass, and the true common ones be restored.

MAN'S JUDGMENT AND GODS

"But with me it is a very small thing that I should be judged of you, or of man's judgment."

FIRST, WE MUST understand Paul's language here, and explain the terms of the original, with which we need to be as familiar as with our mother tongue. He employs the word "judge," or sentence, in a worthy sense; that is, as carrying the thought of esteem. "Judgment," as generally understood, conveys the idea of condemnation. But this is true: every public judgment operates in two ways. One party is condemned, the other liberated; one is punished, the other rewarded; one dishonored, the other honored. The same is true in private judgment. While the Pharisee in the Gospel praised himself, he censured the publican and others; while he honored himself, he dishonored others. And the attitude of everyone toward his neighbor is either praise or censure. Judgment must involve these two things. Hence, Paul here says he is judged, or sentenced, by the Corinthians; that is, their judgment renders honor and praise unto him. By extolling Paul above the other apostles, decision is made between him and the others, to his advantage and with prejudice against them. Some, however, judged in favor of Peter, others of Apollos. That "judgment" is here equivalent to "praise" is evident from the conclusion of the passage: "Judge nothing before the time, until the Lord come, then shall each man have his praise from God." What is this but saying, Praise not, let God praise? It is God's prerogative to judge, to praise and to crown man; we are not to perform that office for one another.

The expression "man's judgment" ("menschliche Tag") implies that judgment of approval whereby man exalts and makes illustrious and renowned those he esteems. The thought is suggestive of the illumination or glory of day, which renders visible things unrevealed in darkness. In the Latin, illustrious people—they who are on everyone's tongue—are called "præclari," "nobiles," "illustres." In German, "durchlauchtige" stands for those of high renown, those having name and reputation superior to others. On the other hand, the unrenowned are called "obscuri," "ignobles," "humiles"—insignificant, unknown, humble.

The holy Scriptures term kings and princes "doxas," "glorious," "claritates," indicative of glory, splendor, and popularity. Peter (2 Pet. 2:10) says of the Pope and his adherents that they tremble not to rail at glories. That means they will curse dignitaries—kings, princes, and all exalted in earthly glory; this when Christ has commanded us to love our enemies, to bless them that curse us, to do good to our persecutors. We see how the Pope defames on Maundy-Thursday in the "Bulla Cænae Domini"; and, indeed, whenever it pleases him.

Man's judgment, then, is expressed in the clamor and ostentation men make before the world. Jeremiah says (17:16), "Neither have I desired the woeful day; thou knowest." In other words, "They accuse me of preaching new doctrines solely to gain a name, and honor and praise before men; to win their esteem. But thou knowest it is not so; I have not sought such honor and praise." Christ says (John 5:41), "I receive not glory from men." That is, "I do not desire men to laud and extol me." And (John 8:50), "I seek not mine own glory." Again (John 5:35), speaking of John the Baptist, "Ye were willing to rejoice for a season in his light." The meaning is, "It would have pleased you to have

John's testimony contribute to your honor and praise; you would have liked to enjoy for a short season the esteem of the people. This is what you sought."

Paul regards it a very trivial matter to command the clamorous honor and praise of men, to gain a reputation with them. He aptly calls such popularity "man's judgment," or human glory. For it is of human origin and not directed of God; and, with men, it shall pass. Paul would say, "I do not desire your praise, nor the praise of all the world." Let men seek for that. Servants of Christ and stewards of God look to Christ and to a divine glory for their judgment.

But the apostle surely manifests ingratitude in not sending the Corinthians a bagful of bulls or letters; in not blessing them nor distributing indulgences among them in recognition of their great honoring of the apostolic see. The Pope would have conducted himself in a manner much more worthy of an apostle. Yes, indeed; he would have anathematized them had they not illumined him with the glory of their judgment. He would have said, "I am a Catholic; the Pope is the highest, the holiest, the mightiest." Had Paul so desired he might have become pope, might have held supremacy; he had but to utter a single word. He had only to receive them who desired to join themselves to him; the others would have been obliged to yield. But in his stewardship he strove for faithfulness rather than for exaltation. Hence he had to remain a common tent-maker and to travel on foot.

From this verse, clearly the Corinthians judged with distinction of persons, preferring that baptism and Gospel which they had themselves received. They intimated that Paul, or Peter, or Apollos, was supreme. This Paul could not admit. He holds the apostles equal, whatever their individualities. He who is baptized and taught by Paul is as much a Christian as one baptized and taught of Peter, or Apollos, or anyone else. In opposition to this teaching, the Pope fiercely rants, admitting no one a Christian unless instructed of himself. At the same time he teaches mere infidelity and the foolish works of men.

Now, Paul condemns undue respect of persons, and in the matter of stewardship for God is concerned only about faithfulness. By these very teachings, he removes every reason for divisions; his Church cannot be disunited, but must remain harmonious, allowing equality in all things. How can there be divisions when one minister of Christ is like another, when he is equally a steward of God? So long as there is no difference in privilege, even if one does exceed another in faithfulness, it will not create sects; it will only publish the common Gospel with greater efficiency.

Paul's words have reference not to one apostle only, but to every apostle. He does not say, "Let a man so account of me," but "Let a man so account of us;" of "us," mark you. Who is meant by "us"? Himself, Peter, Apollos—they about whom the matter arose. The conclusion necessarily is that Peter and Paul are to be considered equal. Then either Paul's teaching is wrong when he regards all apostles equal servants of Christ and stewards of God, or the claims and proceedings of the Pope must be false and this text a powerful enemy of papal pretensions.

"Yea, I judge not mine own self."

You may inquire how it is that Paul should look upon his own judgment of himself as truer than the judgment of any other; for we see how the majority of men praise or highly approve themselves. Naturally one is pleased with himself, but few receive the glory of "man's judgment"—are honored in the sentence of others. We might expect Paul to reverse the statement, saying, "With me it is a very small thing that I should judge myself; I desire neither this human glory of man's judgment, nor the praise of yourselves or of all the world." But he speaks, rather, as a Christian and according to the state of his own conscience before God. The Corinthians exalted Paul in the things acceptable to God. They insisted he was higher, greater and better before God than the other apostles; but certain other Christians extolled Peter.

Now, there is with God no better evidence of the soul's condition than what the conscience reveals. God judges not, like men, according to appearance, but according to the heart; as we learn from 1 Samuel

16:7, "Man looketh on the outward appearance, but Jehovah looketh on the heart." So it is plain the evidence of our consciences is of greater weight before God than the testimony of all the world. And this evidence alone will stand; as said in Romans 2:15, "Their conscience bearing witness therewith, and their thoughts one with another accusing or else excusing them; in the day when God shall judge the secrets of men."

Paul would ask, "Why should divisions arise among you concerning us? What if one is preferred of men before another? It is altogether immaterial. For even our own consciences refrain from judging as to who ranks first in God's sight." Solomon says, "He that trusteth in his own heart is a fool" (Prov. 28:26). There are no grounds for divisions. No one knows who ranks first with God. Christ himself does not claim the right to set one soul on the right hand and the other on the left (Matt. 20:23). Since all the apostles are alike before God, since one is a minister of Christ as well as another, and since we may not know who ranks first in God's estimation, let no one presume to judge, much less to exalt himself above another because of temporal power, wealth or popularity. The exaltation of the Pope and the claim that his eminence is from God is in violation of this principle; Paul's words dispute it, teaching that no one is able to know nor judge until the last day.

But here the keen tongues of the Catholics seek to effect a breach. They assume that Paul does not deny the supremacy of Peter, or of the Pope, but forbids judgment of the person himself as to how good or bad he is in God's sight. I admit that Paul does forbid such judgment, nevertheless the design of the Corinthians for which he rebukes them was to exalt the office, the baptism and the doctrine, wholly because of the person; otherwise they would not have said, "I am a good follower of Paul," "I am a good follower of Peter," and so on. Well they knew that doctrine, baptism and office were the same with all the apostles, but their object was to exalt the office and its efficacy with the standing of the individual. Paul, however, takes the opposite stand; he assumes equality of office upon the very ground of equality of individuals in man's sight, since none can know another's standing before God. Had the Corinthians desired to exalt the individual only, and not the office, they would not have created sects and said, "I am of Paul," etc. Just as we may hold St. Peter holier in person than St. Augustine and yet not cause division thereby. But it is creating sects for one to say, "I am of Peter," and another, "I am of Augustine," meaning, "The doctrine taught me is superior to what is taught you."

The hypocritical Catholics, being well aware that their false claim for the supremacy of the Pope cannot stand unless backed by his personal holiness, proceed to bolster up that falsehood by a greater one. They endeavor to give him the reputation of personal goodness by saying he cannot err, for the Holy Spirit never forsakes him, and Christ is ever with and in him. Some of them, knowing the absurdity of denying that the Pope does openly sin, are so bold in their blasphemous utterances as to declare it is impossible for him to remain in mortal sins for a quarter of an hour. Thus accurately have they measured with hour-glass and compasses the extent of the Holy Spirit's presence in the Pope. Why do they tell such blasphemous falsehoods? Doubtless because they are aware of the futility of attempting to maintain supremacy without personal goodness; they would be compelled to admit that exaltation without piety must be of the devil. It cannot be said the Corinthians exalted the person independently of the office; it was because of his office.

Do you ask further concerning Paul, who desired to be regarded a minister of Christ and a steward of God, Why did he not judge himself? I reply: As before stated, the ministry and the office are not his but God's, who enjoined them upon him. As no man can create the Word of God, so no man has authority to send it forth, or constitute an apostle. God has himself accomplished the work; he has constituted the apostles. Hence we should own the work, glory in it, confess it, and give to publish abroad the news of the priceless blessing the one God has bestowed. To illustrate: Though I cannot constitute myself a living soul, I ought to glory in and confess the fact that God has created me a human being. But just as I am incapable of judging how I stand and will stand in the sight of God, so I cannot judge which apostle or steward is greatest before God.

But you object: You teach, however, that a Christian should not doubt his acceptance with God, and he that doubts is no Christian; for faith assures that God is our Father and that as we believe so shall it be unto us. I reply: Indeed, I would have you hold fast the assurance of faith in the grace of God; faith is simply a steadfast, indubitable, sure confidence in divine grace. But this is what I say: the Corinthians' intent was to judge the apostles by their personal goodness and works, that according to one's holiness, rank and merit might his office be exalted and his followers secure some honor above others. But Paul overthrows all works and merit, leaving them to God's judgment, and places every apostle in the same rank as to office and faith. They fill one and the same office and are justified by one and the same faith. The question of who ranks first in goodness, position, merit and achievement must be left to God; it is not an occasion for divisions in the community. Hence follows:

"For I know nothing against myself; yet am I not hereby justified."

This verse also implies that the Corinthians judged the apostles in regard to the worthiness of person and works; Paul admits his conscience does not reproach him, and confesses to the truth of their judgment so far as his person and conscience are concerned. But, he teaches that such judgment does not suffice before God; and that all decisions based on the same principle are false.

Much might be said on this verse. It shows us all works are rejected and no one is made godly and happy by any of them. The fact that Paul dared say, "I know nothing against myself" proves him certainly to have abounded in good works; nevertheless he says, "I am not hereby justified." By what is he justified, then? By faith alone. Could one be justified upon the grounds of a clear conscience—knowing nothing against himself—his confidence would rest in himself. He could judge and extol his own character, as do presumptuous saints. Then faith and

God's grace would be unnecessary; we would have in ourselves all essentials and could easily dispense with God. The fact is, however, all depends on our reliance upon the grace of God. Thereby are we justified. The subsequent judgment of our works and character, of our calling and worthiness, must be left to God. We are certain we are vindicated by none of these things, and uncertain how God will estimate them.

It is easily evident to all, I presume, that Paul refers to his character after conversion when he says he knows nothing against himself; for, concerning his previous life, he tells us (1 Tim. 1:13) he was an unbeliever, a blasphemer and a persecutor of the first Christians.

The question, however, arises, How can it be that he is not justified by his clear conscience when he declares (2 Cor. 1:12), "For our glorying is this, the testimony of our conscience, that in holiness and sincerity of God, not in fleshly wisdom but in the grace of God, we behaved ourselves in the world, and more abundantly to you-ward"? This quotation contains the answer. The words, "in the grace of God," give it. We are indeed to rejoice in the grace of God, to boast of and glory in it; since it is founded upon the glorying of our conscience. Even had not these words been included, it must necessarily be understood that reference is to the glorying in grace or else to honor before the world.

It is the privilege and the duty of everyone to acknowledge before men his innocence, to rejoice in having injured no one. And he should not call evil what he knows to be good. At the same time such glorying avails nothing before God; he must judge the heart, though men are satisfied with deeds. Before God, then, something more than a good conscience is necessary. Moses says (Ex. 34:7), "Forgiving iniquity and transgression and sin; and that will by no means clear the guilty." We read (Rom. 3:27), "Where then is the glorying?" And again (1 Cor. 1:31), "He that glorieth, let him glory in the Lord"; that is, in his grace.

"But he that judgeth me is the Lord."

The thought here is, "I will wait for God's judgment and praise." Paul says also (2 Cor. 10:18), "For not he that commendeth himself is approved, but whom the Lord commendeth." His intent, however, is not to deter them from godly living but rather to incite thereto. Although no man is capable of judging and commending another, yet none shall go unjudged and uncommended. God himself will judge and praise right living. We should be so much the more faithful in doing good because God is to be judge; we are not to be remiss here even though uncertain as to how he judges us.

"Wherefore judge nothing before the time, until the Lord come, who will both bring to light the hidden things of darkness, and make manifest the counsels of the hearts; and then shall each man have praise of God."

We may well ask, Are we not to give praise to one another? Paul says (Rom. 12:10), "In love of the brethren be tenderly affectioned one to another." And Christ (Matt. 5:16), "Even so let your light shine before men; that they may see your good works, and glorify your Father who is in heaven." And the apostle also tells us (2 Cor. 6:8) we must here upon earth walk "by evil report and good report." But, we reply our faith alone, not our works, is the chief thing to be honored in all cases. Good works are imperative, and we should extol them in others; but no one is to be judged, justified or preferred because of them. The farmer at his plow sometimes may be better in God's sight than the chaste nun.

The five foolish virgins (Matt. 25:2), despite their virginity, are condemned. The widow who threw into the treasury two mites (Mark 12:42) did more than all the others who cast in much greater amounts. The work of the woman who was a sinner (Luke 7:37) is extolled above any work of the Pharisees. It is impossible for us mortals to discern the relative merits of individuals and the value of their works; we ought to praise all, giving equal honors and not preferring one above another. We should humble ourselves before one another, ever esteeming our neighbor above ourselves. Then we are to leave it to God to judge who ranks first. True, he has declared that whoever humbles himself shall be exalted, yet it is not evident who humbles and who exalts himself; for the heart, by which God judges, is not manifest. One may humble himself when secretly in his heart he is haughty, and again the meek-hearted may exalt himself.

So Paul says, "The Lord comes, who will both bring to light the hidden things of darkness, and make manifest the counsels of the hearts." Then it will appear who is really worthier, superior and better, and whose works excel.

It is most unchristian-like to base our estimation of one upon his outward appearance and visible works; to say, for instance, that the Carthusian leads a life essentially better than the farmer, or than any married man. Indeed, the Carthusian if he does right will esteem his own life inferior to that of the married man. For God judges not according to outward expression, but according to the secrets of darkness and the counsels of the heart, and how can the Carthusian know which is the humbler and holier, his own heart or the farmer's?

Applicable here are two instances, in my opinion the best in all the "Lives of the Fathers." One is of St. Anthony, to whom it was revealed that a tanner at Alexandria, a humble, honest mechanic, but one in no wise illustrious, was far superior to the saint because of his humility of heart. The other relates to Paphnutio, who, despite all his austerity of life, was not superior to a fifer nor to either of two married women. It was a special manifestation of grace that God revealed these two incidents at a time when monastic life was most intense, and works prodigious. His purpose was to deter us from judging by outward appearances—by works—and to teach us to value all works alike and to prefer others above ourselves.

Now you will say: If all stations are alike and all works of the same value, none to have preference, what advantage is it to us to forsake the world and enter the holiest orders, to become monks, nuns and priests in the effort to serve God? I reply: Did not Christ and Paul foretell that false Christs and prophets should arise and deceive many? Had the doctrine of equal service to God under all conditions and in all works continued to stand, certainly no monasteries and cloisters would have been established—or at least they would not have increased so rapidly—

to create the illusion that service to God consists only in meeting their requirements. Who would have become a priest, who a monk, yes, who a pope and bishop, had he realized that in such capacity his position and its works are no more meritorious than those of the poorest nurse maid who rocks children and washes swaddling clothes?

It would grievously distress, yes, and shame, the Pope had he to humble himself to a nurse maid, esteeming his works inferior to hers—he whose position and works are so meritorious that kings, and even God's saints, are scarce worthy to kiss his feet. The holy Catholics, then, must institute something superior to Paul's teaching here. They are compelled to judge themselves, and to proclaim their position and works supreme, else they cannot sell their merits and procure heaven for poor laymen, married persons and individuals in various stations, implying that these do not in their lives serve God.

Now, seeing how impossible it is for the present ecclesiastical order to stand unless it disposes of this passage from Paul and exalts its religious life with distinction above that of other Christians, it is certainly clear enough that Catholicism, with its monasteries and cloisters, is based on mere falsehoods and blasphemies. The Catholics style themselves "ecclesiastical" or "spiritual" and others "secular," when God sees none as ecclesiasts or churchmen, but as believers; and believers are found for the most part not among the clergy but among the laity. What greater deception than to call the clerical order spiritual, and to separate it from the class among whom true spiritual life exists? God alone is to judge who is holiest and best. The clerical order assumes the title "spiritual" simply because they have shaved heads and wear long cloaks. What folly—even insanity!

You will say: If this be true, it were better for us to leave the cloisters and monasteries. I reply: There are but two things for you. Follow the teaching of this lesson, commending not yourselves. Regard your order and station no better than as if you were not an ecclesiastic, and your chastity not superior to that of an honest, loyal wife and mother; if you are not willing so to humble your ecclesiasticism, then discard caps, bald pates, cloisters and all. Either adopt this course or know that your ecclesiasticism, your spirituality, has its origin, not with a good spirit, but with an evil spirit. You will never overthrow Paul's doctrine here. It is better to be a mother among the common believers in Christ than to remain a virgin in the devil's cause. Paul stands firm on the point that we must not judge ourselves.

But you will loudly object: Jerome and many others have highly commended virginity; and Paul, too (1 Cor. 7:38), teaches it is better to be a virgin than to marry. I answer: Let Jerome be here or there, Augustine here or Ambrose there, you have learned what God here says through Paul, that no one shall judge 4iimself or anyone else to be best. God's command should have more weight than the sayings of many Jeromes, were they as numerous as the sand grains upon the seashore or the leaves of the forest. True, Paul says it is better to be continent than to marry, but he does not say "in God's sight." If he did, it would be a contradiction of his words here. He who lives continently, it is true, is freer to publish the Gospel than the married man; and it was with the thought of Gospel furtherance that Paul applauded virginity, or continence. He says: "He that is unmarried is careful for the things of the Lord" (1 Cor. 7:32).

Christ also applauds the eunuchs (Matt. 19:12), not for the sake of their condition but for the sake of their profit to the kingdom of heaven; that is, for the sake of their furtherance of the Gospel. Now, although none cares less for the Gospel than do these ecclesiasts, they continue to exalt their position above that of others, and to extol continence for the mere sake of the merit in denial, not for the end it serves. To illustrate the advantage of continence: It is better to learn a trade than to be a servant; and why? Not because it is a condition more acceptable to God, but because it offers less hindrances to his service. It is in this light that Paul applauds virginity and continence; but only in those who have a desire for it through the grace of God.

At present no one cares whether continence is a help or a hindrance; everyone plunges into it, thinking only of how exalted, worthy and great it makes them. All is done with such pains and danger, unwillingness and impurity, that an adequate cry and protest cannot be raised against the evil. Still they wish to be better than other people. Thus they have brought such reproach upon the marriage state that it is considered an impure and disgraceful life. As a reward God permits their continence to pollute their garments and beds continually. Really there is no greater or more polluted incontinence than theirs, inordinate, imprisoned, restrained and intolerable as it is.

"Bring to light the hidden things of darkness, and make manifest the counsels of the hearts."

Paul gives the reason we should refrain from commending ourselves or any other when he declares that the hidden things of darkness and the counsels of the hearts are not yet brought to light. Since God judges according to the secrets of the heart which we cannot know, we should withhold judgment of the various stations and works of men, and not make distinction. The virgin is not to exalt her state of virginity above the station of the wife. The Pope ought to humble his eminence below the position of the plow-boy. No one should presume to regard his own station, or that of another, as better before God than the occupations of other men.

Every person should be free to choose and live in the state that suits him, all being alike until the Lord comes. But, were this principle to be carried out where would the holy fathers and the spiritual lords obtain their daily bread, not being accustomed to labor? They secure their subsistence by making the impression that the common man is in error and by separating from him their states and position. They judge themselves to be the best people, confident of enjoying the common man's treasures, because his state is nothing. Hence arise so many institutions, and gifts flow to the cloisters, chapels and churches for the especial benefit of these idle, beloved gluttons and gormandizers. All this would fall were Paul's teachings introduced.

By the "hidden things of darkness" and the "counsels of the hearts" Paul refers to the two powers commonly but not very intelligibly termed "will" and "reason." Man possesses in his inmost being two capacities: he loves, delights, desires, wills; and he understands, perceives, judges, decides. I shall term these capacities "motive" and "thought."

The motives and desires of man are deep and deceitful beyond recognition; no saint, even, can wholly comprehend them. Jeremiah says (17:9-10), "The heart is deceitful above all things, and it is exceedingly corrupt: who can know it? I, Jehovah, search the mind, I try the heart." And David (Ps. 32:2), "Blessed is the man in whose spirit there is no guile."

Many pious individuals perform great works from a selfish motive or desire. They seek their own interests, yet never with assurance. They serve God not purely for love of him, but for the sake of personal honor or profit; of, gaining heaven and escaping the tortures of hell. One cannot realize the falseness of his motives until God permits him to endure many severe temptations. So Paul calls such motives "hidden things of darkness," a most appropriate name. Not only are they concealed, but in darkness, in the inmost heart, where they are unperceived by the individual himself and known to God alone.

Remembering this deplorable secret motive of the heart, we should be induced to submit ourselves one to another and not to contrast any particular work or station with others. The motive determines the force and judgment of every work, every station, of all conduct, of every life. As Solomon says (Prov. 16:2), "Jehovah weigheth the spirits"—God is the weigh-master of the spirits. Since there may be something of good concealed in the secret heart of the wife and likewise something of evil in the virgin's heart, it is absurd and unchristian to exalt a virgin above a wife because of her continence, a purely external virtue. It is just as unreasonable to measure the two by their external life as to compare the weight of eggs by putting the shells into the balance and leaving out the contents.

Now, according to our secret motives so are our thoughts—good or evil. Our motives and desires control our aims, decisions and reasonings. These latter Paul terms "counsels of the heart"—the thoughts we arrive at in consequence of our secret motives and desires.

Of these two, Mary hints in her song of praise (Luke 1:51), "He hath scattered the proud in the imagination of their heart." She calls intent or motive of the heart the "hidden things of darkness"—her desire, while the "counsels" and imaginations are the heart's expression. Moses, referring to man's heart, says (Gen. 6:5), "Every imagination of the thoughts of his heart was only evil continually." And Christ (Matt. 6:22-23) earnestly warns us against the same false motive,

> "The lamp of the body is the eye: if therefore thine eye be single, thy whole body shall be full of light. But if thine eye be evil, thy whole body shall be full of darkness. If therefore the light that is in thee be darkness, how great is the darkness!"

The reference in this whole quotation is to the secret workings of darkness, which are not to be overcome in any way but by despair of our own works, and strong faith in the pure grace of God. Nothing is more conducive to this end than sufferings severe and many, and all manner of misfortunes. Under such influences man may learn, to some extent, to know himself; otherwise all is lost.

4

Fourth Sunday in Advent

"Rejoice in the Lord always: again I will say, Rejoice. Let your forbearance be known unto all men. The Lord is at hand. In nothing be anxious; but in everything by prayer and supplication with thanksgiving let your requests be made known unto God. And the peace of God, which passeth all understanding, shall guard your hearts and your thoughts in Christ Jesus" (Philippians 4:4-7).

THE TEXT, THOUGH short, is a suggestive and important lesson in Christian faith. It teaches how we should conduct ourselves toward God and our neighbor. It says:

"Rejoice in the Lord always."

OUR CONDUCT TOWARD GOD— REJOICE IN HIM

JOY IS THE NATURAL fruit of faith. The apostle says elsewhere (Gal. 5:22-23), "The fruit of the Spirit is love, joy, peace, longsuffering, kindness, goodness, faithfulness, meekness, self-control." Until the heart believes in God, it is impossible for it to rejoice in him. When faith is lacking, man is filled with fear and gloom and is disposed to flee at the very mention, the mere thought, of God. Indeed, the unbelieving heart is filled with enmity and hatred against God. Conscious of its own guilt, it has no confidence in his gracious mercy; it knows God is an enemy to sin and will terribly punish the same.

Since there exist in the heart these two things—a consciousness of sin and a perception of God's chastisement—the heart must ever be depressed, faint, even terrified. It must be continually apprehensive that

God stands behind ready to chastise. Solomon says (Prov. 28:1), "The wicked flee when no man pursueth." And Deuteronomy 28:65-66 reads, "Jehovah will give thee there a trembling heart . . . . and thy life shall hang in doubt." One may as well try to persuade water to burn as to talk to such a heart of joy in God. All words will be without effect, for the sinner feels upon his conscience the pressure of God's hand. The prophet's injunction (Ps. 32:11) likewise is: "Be glad in Jehovah, and rejoice, ye righteous; and shout for joy, all ye that are upright in heart." It must be the just and the righteous who are to rejoice in the Lord. This text, therefore, is written, not for the sinner, but for the saint. First we must tell sinners how they can be liberated from their sins and perceive a merciful God. When they have been released from the power of an evil conscience, joy will result naturally.

But how shall we be liberated from an accusing conscience and receive the assurance of God's mercy? The question has been sufficiently answered in the preceding postils, and will be again frequently satisfied later on. He who would have a quiet conscience, and would be sensitive of God's mercy, must not, like the apostates, depend on works, still further doing violence to the heart and increasing its hatred of God. He must place no hope whatever in works; must apprehend God in Christ, comprehend the Gospel and believe its promises.

But what does the Gospel promise other than that Christ is given for us; that he bears our sins; that he is our Bishop, Mediator, and Advocate before God, and that thus only through him and his work is God reconciled, are our sins forgiven and our consciences set free and made glad? When this sort of faith in the Gospel really exists in the heart, God is recognized as favorable and pleasing. The heart confidently feels his favor and grace, and only these. It fears not God's chastisement. It is secure and in good spirit because God has conferred upon it, through Christ, superabundant goodness and grace. Essentially, the fruits of such a faith are love, peace, joy, and songs of thanksgiving and praise. It will enjoy unalloyed and sincere pleasure in God as its supremely beloved and gracious Father, a Father whose attitude toward itself has been wholly paternal, and who, without any merit on its part, has richly poured out upon that heart his goodness.

Such is the rejoicing, mark you, of which Paul here speaks—a rejoicing where is no sin, no fear of death or hell, but rather a glad and all-powerful confidence in God and his kindness. Hence the expression, "Rejoice in the Lord"; not rejoice in silver or gold, not in eating or drinking, not in pleasure or mechanical chanting, not in strength or health, not in skill or wisdom, not in power or honor, not in friendship or favor, nay, not in good works or holiness even. For these are deceptive joys, false joys, which never stir the depths of the heart. They are never even felt. When they are present we may well say the individual rejoices superficially, and without a heart experience.

To rejoice in the Lord—to trust, confide, glory and have pride in the Lord as in a gracious Father—this is a joy which rejects all else but the Lord, including that self-righteousness whereof Jeremiah speaks (9:23-24),

> "Let not the wise man glory in his wisdom, neither let the mighty man glory in his might, let not the rich man glory in his riches; but let him that glorieth glory in this, that he hath understanding, and knoweth me."

Again, Paul enjoins (2 Cor. 10:17), "He that glorieth, let him glory in the Lord."

The apostle further commands in our text to rejoice "always." Thus he rebukes those who rejoice in God—who praise and thank him—only a portion of the time. These rejoice when it is well with them; when not, rejoicing ceases. Concerning them Psalm 48 teaches, they will praise God when he favors them. David does not so. He declares (Ps. 34:1), "I will bless Jehovah at all times; his praise shall continually be in my mouth." And David has good reason to do so, for who will harm or distress one favored of God? Sin harms him not; nor death nor hell. David sings (Ps. 23:4), "Yea, though I walk through the valley of the shadow of death, I will fear no evil." And Paul queries (Rom. 8:35), "Who shall separate us from the love of Christ? shall tribulation, or anguish, or persecution, or famine, or nakedness, or peril, or sword?"

And then he goes on (verses 38-39): "For I am persuaded, that neither death, nor life, nor angels, nor principalities, nor things present, nor things to come, nor powers, nor height, nor depth, nor any other creature, shall be able to separate us from the love of God, which is in Christ Jesus our Lord." "Again I will say, Rejoice."

The apostle emphasizes his admonition by repeating it. It is essential that we rejoice. Paul, recognizing that we live in the midst of sin and evil, both which things depress, would fortify us with cheer. Thus rejoicing, even if we should sometimes fall into sin, our joy in God will exceed our sorrow in sin. The natural accompaniment of sin truly is fear and a burdened conscience, and we cannot always escape sin. Therefore we should let joy have rule, let Christ be greater than our sins. John says (1 John 2:1-2), "If any man sin, we have an Advocate with the Father, Jesus Christ the righteous; and he is the propitiation for our sins." Again (1 John 3:20), "Because if our heart condemn us, God is greater than our heart, and knoweth all things."

OUR CONDUCT TO MAN—FORBEARANCE

"Let your forbearance [moderation] be known unto all men."

HAVING INSTRUCTED THE Corinthians concerning their conduct toward God—their duty to serve him with joyful hearts—Paul proceeds briefly to teach them how to conduct themselves before men, saying, "Let your moderation be known unto all men." In other words: Rejoice always before God, but before men be forbearing. Direct your life so as to do and suffer everything not contrary to the commandments of God, that you may make yourselves universally agreeable. Not only refrain from offending any, but put the best possible construction upon the conduct of others. Aim to be clearly recognized as men indifferent to circumstances, as content whether you be hit or missed, and holding to no privilege at all liable to bring you into conflict or produce discord. With the rich be rich; with the poor, poor. Rejoice with the joyful, weep with the mourning. Finally, be all things to all men, compelling them to confess you always agreeable, uniformly pleasant to mankind and on a level with everyone.

Such is the meaning of the little word here employed by the apostle—"epiikia," equity, clemency, accommodation—and which we cannot better render than by "moderation" or "forbearance." It is the virtue of adapting or accommodating oneself to another; of endorsing that other; of making all equal; of presenting a like attitude toward all men; not setting oneself up as a model and pattern; not desiring mankind to do homage to one, to conform to one's position. Justice may be classified as severe and mild. Too severe justice is often mitigated, and that is the equity, the moderation and clemency of the law. The Latin translator has rendered our word "modestiam," "moderation." This word would properly convey the thought were it not generally understood in its relation to eating, drinking and dressing. Here the intent is to indicate that moderation of life which adjusts and adapts self to the abilities and circumstances of others, yielding, commending, following, mitigating, doing, allowing, forbearing, according as one recognizes what the capacity and condition of a neighbor demands, even to the disparagement of one's own honor and life, and the detriment of his possessions.

For the sake of a better understanding, let us illustrate: Paul says (1 Cor. 9:19-22),

> "For though I was free from all men, I brought myself under bondage to all, that I might gain the more. And to the Jews I became as a Jew, that I might gain Jews; to them that are under the law, as under the law, not being myself under the law, that I might gain them that are under the law; to them that are without law, as without law, not being without law to God, but under law to Christ, that I might gain them that are without law . . . I am become all things to all men, that I may by all means save some."

That is, Paul ate and drank with the Jews according to the law, and generally conducted himself in harmony with its requirements; though he was not obliged so to do. He also ate and drank with the gentiles regardless of the law, and conducted himself without respect to its requirements and as the custom of the gentiles. For only faith and love are requisite. All else man is free to omit or to observe. Therefore, for the sake of one, all laws may be observed; for another, omitted. Observance must be adapted to the individual case.

Now, suppose some blind, capricious individual intrudes, demanding as necessary the omission of this thing and the observance of that, as did certain Jews, and insisting that all men follow him and he none—this would be to destroy equality; indeed, even to exterminate Christian liberty and faith. Like Paul, in the effort to maintain liberty and truth, everyone should refuse to yield to any such demand.

To illustrate further: Christ suffered his disciples to break the Sabbath—and himself frequently broke it— where necessary (Matt. 12 and Mark 2); but where necessity did not require otherwise, he observed the day. He assigned as reason for his conduct, "The Son of man is lord even of the sabbath" (Mark 2:28). That is, the law of the Sabbath permits freedom; for the sake of extending love and service to one, it may be broken; and to another, it may be observed.

Because of the Jews, Luke says, Paul circumcised Timothy. But he would not permit Titus to be circumcised for the very reason that false brethren insisted upon it and were unwilling to concede it a matter of choice. Paul claimed authority both to observe circumcision and not to observe it, according as would best contribute to the benefit of others. He deemed neither one course nor the other necessary. He did not believe in circumcision for the sake of the work itself—as a thing which must be performed.

But to make the application to ourselves: When the Pope commands us to confess, to receive the sacrament, to fast, to eat fish, or to perform any bidding of his, and insists that we must do these things because the Church requires it of us, we should calmly trample upon his injunctions, doing what is directly opposed, simply to defy him and maintain liberty. But when he does not insist upon these things, we should honor his desire by observing with observers and omitting with those who omit, presenting Christ's testimony, "The Son of man is lord even of the sabbath," and declaring him much more Lord of human laws. To exercise our liberty in the observance of these commands, works no harm to faith nor to the Gospel; but to observe them by a forced act of obedience, destroys faith and the Gospel.

The same rule applies to all external institutions and ordinances, as monastic vows and rules. They are in themselves but a matter of choice and are not opposed to faith or love. We should maintain the privilege of observing them in love and liberty, for the sake of our associates—to preserve harmony with them. But when it is insisted that certain ordinances must be honored, that their observance is an act of obedience essential to salvation, we should forsake cloisters, tonsures, caps, vows and rules, and even take the opposite course, by way of testifying that only faith and love are the Christian essentials and it is our privilege to observe or omit all other things, being controlled by love and our associations. To conform to laws in a spirit of love and liberty works no harm, but to conform through necessity and forced obedience is to be condemned. Let this rule apply to ceremonials, hymns, prayers and all other Cathedral ordinances, so long as they are observed as a matter of love and liberty alone. Only for the service and for the enjoyment of the assembled company are they to be observed, and that when they are works not in themselves evil. When urged as inherently essential, we are to refrain; we must oppose them in order to maintain the liberty of faith.

Herein you see the diabolical character of the papal institutions, cloisters, in fact all Roman Catholicism. For they simply make a matter of liberty and love one of necessity and forced obedience, whereby the Gospel, faith included, is exterminated, not to mention the consequent wretchedness of the common people who submit to obey for the sake of their, appetites. For how many now attend the choral ceremonies and pray specified hours for God's sake? A general destruction of cloisters and other institutions would be the best reformation in this respect. They are of no benefit to Christianity and might easily be dispensed with. Before liberty could be established in one such institution, a hundred thousand souls might be lost in the others. When a thing is not beneficial and serves no purpose, but does unspeakable injury, and is beyond remedy, it is much better to utterly exterminate it.

But again, when civil government enjoins laws and demands tribute, we should freely serve, even though we are constrained. In this case our liberty and faith are not endangered. For civil government does not claim that observance of its laws is essential to salvation, but essential to civil dominion and protection. In submitting to it, then, conscience maintains its liberty, and faith is not impaired. To whatever does not do violence to our faith, and benefits others, we should fully conform. But when it is insisted that observation of any material laws is essential to salvation, our course of action should be the same as that already suggested relative to the laws of the Pope and the cloisters.

Now, the illustrations given serve as examples to follow in every instance. As Paul here teaches, let one put himself on an equality with all men, being not content to consider simply his own claims and rights, but the wishes and well-being of others. Paul has here in a single word set aside all rights. If your neighbor's condition really demands that you yield a certain personal right or privilege, and you insist upon that privilege, you act at variance with the principle of love and equality and are indeed blameworthy. For in yielding you sustain no injury to your faith, and your neighbor is profited. You would desire him to do thus unto you—a principle of natural law.

Indeed, we further add, in the event of one working you harm or injury, you are to put the best construction upon his act, excusing it in the spirit of that holy martyr who, when all his possessions were taken from him, said, "Truly, they can never take Christ from me." Say you likewise: "His act injures not my faith; why not excuse him? Why not submit and accommodate myself to him?"

I cannot better illustrate than by citing the conduct of two good friends, whose manner toward each other may serve as an example for us in our conduct toward all men. How did they act? Each did what pleased his fellow. Each yielded, submitted, suffered, wrought, and accepted, just in accordance with his conception of what might profit or please the other, and all voluntarily, without constraint. Each adapted and accommodated himself to his friend, never from any selfish motive offering restraint. If one infringed upon the other's property rights, he was kindly excused. In short, in their case was neither law, demand, restraint, nor fear; naught but perfect freedom and good will. Yet all things moved in a harmony the hundredth part of which could not be secured by any laws or restraints.

The headstrong and the unyielding, they who excuse none but are determined to control all things by their own wisdom, lead the whole world into error. They are the cause of all the wars and calamities known on earth. Yet they claim justice as their sole motive. Well has it been said by a certain heathen: "Summum jus, summa injustitia"—the most extreme justice is the greatest injustice. Ecclesiastes 7:16 also warns, "Be not righteous overmuch; neither make thyself overwise." As the most extreme justice is the greatest injustice, so the most extreme wisdom is the greatest folly. The old adage is, "When the wise act the fool, they are grossly foolish." Were God always to execute extreme justice, we could not live a moment. Paul commends gentleness in Christ (2 Cor. 10:1), saying, "I . . . entreat you by the meekness and gentleness of Christ." So we are to moderate our attitude, our demands, our wisdom and wit, adapting ourselves to the circumstances of others in all respects.

Observe the beautiful aptness of the words, "Let your forbearance be known unto all men." You may ask, "How can one become known to all men? And must we boast of our forbearance, proclaiming it to everyone?" God forbid the latter. Paul does not say, boast of and proclaim your forbearance. He says, let it be experimentally known by all men. That is, exercise forbearance in your deeds before men; not think or speak of it, but show it in your conduct. Thus men generally must see and grasp it—must have experience of it. Then no one can do otherwise than admit you are forbearing. Actual experience will defeat every desire to speak of you in any other way. The mouth of the fault-finder will be stopped by the fact that all men know your forbearance. Christ says (Matt. 5:16): "Even so let your light so shine before men; that they may see your good works, and glorify your Father who is in heaven." And Peter (1 Pet. 2:12): "Having your behavior seemly among the Gentiles;

that, wherein they speak against you as evil-doers, they may by your good works, which they behold, glorify God in the day of visitation." It lies not in our power to make our moderation acceptable to all men, but it is enough for us to give everyone opportunity to perceive it in our lives.

By the phrase "all men" we are not to understand all individuals on earth, but every sort of person—friends and foes, great and humble, lords and servants, rich and poor, native and alien, relatives and strangers. Some there are whose manner toward strangers is most cordial and acquiescent, but toward their own household, their domestics, with whom they are familiar, they manifest only rigor and austerity. How many there are who excuse the harshness of the great and the rich, who wrest to the most favorable construction what they do and say, but with servants, with the poor and the inferior, are severe and unfeeling, placing the most unfavorable construction upon their every word and act. Again, men are affectionate toward children, parents, friends and relatives, always judging them with the utmost lenience. Indeed, how often friend flatters friend, until the practice becomes a public vice as one imitates and regards admirable all acts of the other. But with foes and adversaries men adopt the opposite course. In them they can find no good, no reason for toleration or favorable construction; rather, they censure according to appearances.

In denunciation of such unequal and partial forbearance, Paul here speaks. He would have a Christian's forbearance perfect and complete, manifested toward one as toward another, whether friend or foe. He would that the Christian bear with and excuse everyone, regardless of person or merit. Forbearance is essentially good, inherently kind; just as gold remains gold whether possessed by a godly or an ungodly individual. The silver did not become ashes when Judas the traitor received it. Similarly, all gifts of God are real and remain the same in everyone's possession. That forbearance which is a fruit of the Spirit retains its characteristic kindness whether directed toward friend or enemy, toward rich or poor.

But frail, deceptive human nature assumes that gold, though remaining gold in St. Peter's hand, becomes ashes in the hand of Judas. The forbearance of human nature, of natural reason, is kind, not to all men, but to the rich and the great, to strangers and friends. Hence it is false, empty, deceptive; mere dissimulation and treachery before God. Note how impossible it is for human nature to exercise complete spiritual forbearance, and how few individuals are conscious of the imperfections of that supposedly beautiful, transcendent forbearance they manifest toward some persons while they show the reverse to other individuals, presuming they thus act rightly. But such is the teaching of our mean, filthy human nature with that same beautiful reason, which ever decides and proceeds contrary to the Spirit and the things of the Spirit. As Paul says in Romans 8:5, "They that are after the flesh mind the things of the flesh."

In these few words Paul comprehends the Christian's entire conduct toward his neighbor. The forbearing individual treats everyone rightly, in word and act; treats him as he ought, physically and spiritually, bearing with his evils and imperfections. Such conduct may be defined as simply love, peace, patience, longsuffering, gentleness, goodness, meekness, in fact, everything included in the fruits of the Spirit (Gal. 5:22).

OBJECTIONS ANSWERED

BUT YOU WILL say: "Yes, but in that case who would be left in the enjoyment of a morsel of bread because of the wicked people ready to abuse equality and take our all, not permitting us to live on the earth even?" Note Paul's beautiful answer to your question, in the conclusion of this epistle lesson. He says, first,

"The Lord is at hand."

Were there no God, you might well thus fear the wicked. But not only is there a God; he "is at hand." He will neither forget nor forsake you. Only be forbearing to all men, and let him care for you; leave it to him how he is to support and protect you. Has he given you Christ the eternal treasure? How then shall he not give you the necessities of this life? With him is much more than anyone can take from you. Then, too, you possess in Christ more than is represented in all this world's goods. On this subject the psalmist says (Ps. 55:22), "Cast thy burden upon Jehovah, and he will sustain thee"; and Peter (1 Pet. 5:7), "Casting all your anxiety upon him, because he careth for you." And Christ in the sixth chapter of Matthew points us to the lilies of the field and the fowls of the air. The thought of these passages is the same as that of "The Lord is at hand." Now follows,

"In nothing be anxious."

Take no thought for yourselves. Let God care for you. He whom you now acknowledge is able to provide for you. It is the heathen, unknowing he has a God, who takes thought for himself. Christ says (Matt. 6:31-32),

> "Be not therefore anxious, saying, What shall we eat? or, What shall we drink? or, Wherewithal shall we be clothed? For after all these things do the Gentiles seek; for your heavenly Father knoweth that ye have need of all these things."

Then, let the whole world grasp, and deal unrighteously, you shall have enough. You shall not die of hunger or cold unless someone shall have deprived you of the God who cares for you. But who shall take him from you? How can you lose him except you yourself let him go? We have no reason to take thought for ourselves when we have a Father and Protector who holds in his hand all things, even them who, with all their possessions, would rob or injure us. Our duty is to rejoice ever in God and be forbearing toward all men, as becomes those assured of ample provision for body and soul; especially in that we have a gracious God. They without him may well be concerned about themselves. It should be our anxiety not to be anxious, to rejoice in God alone and to be kind to men. On this topic the psalmist says (Ps. 37:25), "I have been young, and now am old; yet have I not seen the righteous forsaken, nor his seed begging bread." And again (Ps. 40:17), "The Lord thinketh upon me."

PRAYER

"But in everything by prayer and supplication with thanksgiving let your requests be made known unto God."

HERE PAUL TEACHES us to cast our care upon God. The meaning is: Take no thought for yourselves. Should anything transpire to give you care or anxiety—and such will be the case, for many trials will befall you on earth—make no effort to escape it, be it what it may. Have no care or anxiety. Turn to God with prayer, with supplication, entreating him to accomplish for you all you would seek to effect by care. And do so in thankfulness that you have a God solicitous for you and to whom you may freely come with all your anxieties. Who does not so when misfortune befalls, but endeavors to measure it by his reason and to overrule it by his counsel, and falls into anxiety—this man plunges himself into deep wretchedness, loses his joy and peace in God, and all to accomplish nothing. He but digs in the sand, sinking himself ever deeper, and effects no good. Of this fact we daily have testimony in our own experience and in that of others.

It may be necessary to add this, however: Let no one conclude he will be utterly careless and rest upon God, making no effort, no exertion, not even resorting to prayer. Whoso adopts this course must soon fail and fall into anxiety. We must ever strive. Many care-engendering things befall us for the very purpose of driving us to prayer. Not undesignedly does the apostle contrast the two injunctions, "In nothing be anxious," and, "In all things flee to God." "Nothing" and "all" are contrasting terms. Paul thus makes plain that many things transpire which tend to create in us anxiety, but we must not let them make us overanxious; we must commit ourselves to God and implore his aid for our needs.

Now, let us examine Paul's words and learn how to frame our prayers and what attitude to assume. He makes a fourfold division of prayer: prayer, supplication, thanksgiving and petition. By "prayer" we understand simply formal words or expressions—as, for instance, the Lord's Prayer and the psalms—which sometimes express more than our request. In "supplication" we strengthen prayer and make it effective by a certain form of persuasion; for instance, we may entreat one to grant a request for the sake of a father, or of something dearly loved or highly prized. We entreat God by his Son, his saints, his promises, his name. Thus Solomon says (Ps. 132:1), "Jehovah, remember for David all his affliction." And Paul urges (Rom. 12:1), "I beseech you therefore, brethren, by the mercies of God"; and again (2 Cor. 10:1), "I . . . entreat you by the meekness and gentleness of Christ." "Petitioning" is stating what we have at heart, naming the desire we express in prayer and supplication. In the Lord's Prayer are seven petitions, beside prayer proper. Christ says (Matt. 7:7-8), "Ask, and it shall be given you; seek, and ye shall find; knock, and it shall be opened unto you: for every one that asketh receiveth; and he that seeketh findeth; and to him that knocketh it shall be opened." In "thanksgiving" we recount blessings received and thus strengthen our confidence and enable ourselves to wait trustingly for what we pray.

Prayer is made vigorous by petitioning; urgent by supplication; by thanksgiving, pleasing and acceptable. Strength and acceptability combine to prevail and secure the petition. This, we see, is the manner of prayer practiced by the Church; and the holy fathers in the Old Testament always offered supplication and thanks in their prayers. The Lord's Prayer opens with praise and thanksgiving and the acknowledgment of God as a Father; it earnestly presses toward him through filial love and a recognition of fatherly tenderness. For supplication, this prayer is unequaled. Hence it is the sublimest and the noblest prayer ever uttered.

These words of Paul beautifully spiritualize and explain the mystery of the golden censer whereof Moses has written much in the Old Testament, detailing how the priests should burn incense in the temple. We are all priests, and our prayers are the censer. The first is the golden vessel, which signifies the precious words of prayer; such as the language of the Lord's Prayer, the psalms, and like written prayers. Always in the

Scriptures the words are represented by the vessel; for words are a medium for containing and conveying thought, just as the vessel serves to contain wine, water, coals or anything else. Similarly, the golden cup of Babylon mentioned in Revelation 17:4 typifies human doctrine; and the sacramental cup, containing Christ's blood, is the Gospel.

The live coals in the censer stand for thanksgiving, for enumerated benefits in prayer. That coals signify benefits Paul implies where, quoting Solomon's injunction in Proverbs 25:21-22, which the apostle cites (Rom. 12:20), "If thine enemy hunger, feed him; if he thirst, give him to drink; for in so doing thou shalt heap coals of fire upon his head." Burning coals of fire, the benefits are, and powerful to take captive and enkindle the heart. The Law forbad to take coals from any place but the altar; accordingly, we must not in prayer urge our own works and merits, as did the Pharisee in the Gospel (Luke 18:11-12), but acknowledge the benefits in Christ. He is the altar upon whom we are offered. By this benefit we render thanks and pray. Paul says (Col. 3:17), "Do all in the name of the Lord Jesus, giving thanks to God the Father through him." God cannot permit us to regard anything but our altar Christ. Thus he teaches, where it is recorded (Lev. 10) that Nadab and Abihu, sons of Aaron, were devoured by fire before the altar because they took coals for the censer from elsewhere than that place of sacred offering.

The petition whereby prayer is made complete is typified by the smoke ascending at the laying of the thyme—the incense—upon the coals. Paul's exhortation, "Let your requests be made known unto God," recognizes and explains the symbol of the smoke rising from the censer. His meaning is: "If you would offer a sweet savor of incense to God, express your petition in supplication and thanksgiving. This is the precious, sweet incense recognized by God, ascending as straight before him as a taper and a rod." Such prayer penetrates heaven. Grateful recognition of God's benefits induces us to pray voluntarily and fervently, naturally and with delight; just as the coals of fire make strong the volume of smoke. If there be not first the coals to generate heat, if there be not gratitude for benefits to enkindle fervor, prayer will be sluggish; it will be cold and dull.

But what is meant by "making known" our prayers to God when he knows them even before we begin, in fact, comes to us first and induces us to pray? I answer, Paul uses this expression by way of teaching us how to really and truly pray—not to pray vainly or at a venture as do they who are indifferent whether God hears them or not, who are ever uncertain of being heard, yes, are inclined to think they will not be heard. That is not praying; it is not petitioning. It is tempting and mocking God. Should one entreat me for a penny and I knew he did not believe, did not have a thought, that I would give it him, I would not be disposed to hear him. I would conclude he was either mocking me or was not in earnest. How much less will God hear mere noise! True prayer is the "making known" of our desires to God. In other words, we must not doubt that God hears us; that our prayer reaches him; that our requests assuredly shall be granted. If we do not believe we are heard, that our prayer reaches God, undoubtedly it will not reach him. As we believe, so will it be.

The ascending smoke is but our faith when we believe our appeal reaches God and is heard. Paul's words hint at the frequent claims of the psalms: "My cry before him came into his ears" (Ps. 18:6). "Let my prayer be set forth . . . before thee" (Ps. 141:2). Relative to this topic, Christ says, "All things, whatsoever ye shall ask in prayer, believing, ye shall receive" (Matt. 21:22; see also Mark 11:24). And James counsels (1:6-7), "But let him ask in faith, nothing doubting; for he that doubteth . . . let not that man think that he shall receive anything of the Lord."

Easily, then, we recognize the bawling in the cloisters and cathedrals all over the world as mere mockery, a tempting of God. Prayer of that sort is well enough made known to men, considering the constant loud outcry and bellowing of them who offer it. But to God it is unknown. It fails to reach him because the offerers do not believe, or at least are uncertain, that it will. As they believe, so is it. Time indeed it is for such mockery and tempting of God to be rejected and the mockhouses, as Amos calls them in the seventh chapter, to be exterminated.

Oh, if we would but pray aright, what could we not accomplish! As it is, we pray much and obtain nothing; for our prayers never reach God. Wo to unbelief and distrust!

THE PEACE OF GOD

"And the peace of God, which passeth all understanding, shall guard your hearts and your thoughts in Christ Jesus."

NOTE THE BEAUTIFUL logic and order of Paul's teaching. The Christian is first to rejoice in God through faith and then show forbearance or kindness, to men. Should he ask, "How can I?" Paul answers, "The Lord is at hand." "But how if I be persecuted and robbed?" Paul's reply is, "In nothing be anxious. Pray to God. Let him care." "But meanwhile I shall become weary and desolate." "Not so; the peace of God shall keep you." Let us now consider the last thought.

By the phrase, "the peace of God," we must understand, not that calm and satisfied peace wherein God himself dwells, but the peace and contentment he produces in our hearts. It is called the "peace of God" in the same sense that the message of God which we hear and believe and speak is styled "the Word of God." This peace is the gift of God, and is called the "peace of God" because, having it, we are at peace with him even if we are displeased with men.

This peace of God is beyond the power of mind and reason to comprehend. Understand, however, it is not beyond man's power to experience—to be sensible of. Peace with God must be felt in the heart and conscience. How else could our "hearts and minds" be preserved "through Christ Jesus"? To illustrate the difference between the peace of God and the peace comprehensible by reason: They who know nothing of fleeing to God in prayer, when overtaken by tribulation and adversity and when filled with care and anxiety proceed to seek that peace alone which reason apprehends and which reason can secure. But reason apprehends no peace apart from a removal of the evil. Such a peace does not transcend the comprehension of reason; it is compatible with reason. They who pray not, rage and strive under the guidance of reason until they obtain a certain peace by fraudulent or forcible removal of the evil. Just as the wounded seeks to be healed. But they who rejoice in God, finding their peace in him, are contented. They calmly endure tribulation, not desiring what reason dictates as peace—removal of the evil. Standing firm, they await the inner strength wrought by faith. It is not theirs to inquire whether the evil will be short or long in duration, whether temporal or eternal; they give themselves no concern on this point, but ever leave it to God's regulation. They are not anxious to know when, how, where or by whom termination of the evil is to come. In return, God affords them grace and removes their evils, bestowing blessings beyond their expectations, or even desires.

This, mark you, is the peace of the cross, the peace of God, peace of conscience, Christian peace, which gives us even external calm, which makes us satisfied with all men and unwilling to disturb any. Reason cannot understand how there can be pleasure in crosses, and peace in disquietude; it cannot find these. Such peace is the work of God, and none can understand it until it has been experienced. Relative to this topic, it is said in the epistle for the second Sunday in Advent: "The God of hope fill you with all joy and peace in believing." What the apostle there terms "peace in believing" he here calls "peace of God."

In this verse Paul implies that for him who rejoices in God and exercises forbearance in his life, the devil will raise up a cross calculated forcibly to turn his heart from that way. The Christian should therefore be well fortified, placing his peace beyond the devil's reach—in God. Let him not be anxious to rid himself of what the devil has forced upon him. Let him suffer Satan's wantonness until God's coming shall exterminate it. Thus will the Christian's heart, mind and affection be guarded and preserved in peace. His patience could not long endure did not his heart exist above its conditions, in a higher peace—were it not satisfied it has peace with God.

"Heart" and "mind" here must not be supposed to mean human will and understanding. We are to take Paul's explanation—heart and mind in Christ Jesus; in other words, the will and understanding resultant in Christ, from Christ and under Christ. Faith and love are meant—faith and love in all their operations, in all their inclinations toward God and men. The reference is simply to a disposition to trust and love God sincerely, and a willingness of heart and mind to serve God and man to the utmost. The devil seeks to prevent this state by terror, by revealing death and by every sort of misfortune; and by setting up human devices to induce the heart to seek comfort and help in its own counsels and in man. Thus led astray, the heart falls from trust in God to a dependence upon itself.

Briefly, this text is a lesson in Christian living, in the attitude of the Christian toward God and man. It teaches us to let God be everything to us, and to treat all men alike, to conduct ourselves toward men as does God toward us, receiving from him and giving to them. It may be summed up in the words "faith" and "love."

5

First Christmas Sermon

(Christmas Eve Service)

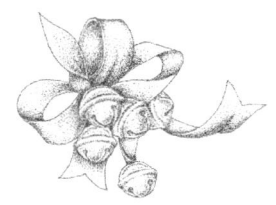

"For the grace of God hath appeared, bringing salvation to all men, instructing us, to the intent that, denying ungodliness and worldly lusts, we should live soberly and righteously and godly in this present world; looking for the blessed hope and appearing of the glory of the great God and our Saviour Jesus Christ; who gave himself for us, that he might redeem us from all iniquity, and purify unto himself a people for his own possession, zealous of good works. These things speak and exhort and reprove with all authority. Let no man despise thee" (Titus 2:11-15).

THE APPEARING OF THE GRACE OF GOD

IT IS WRITTEN IN the book of Nehemiah (chapter 4) that the Jews, in rebuilding Jerusalem, wrought with one hand and with the other held the sword, because of the enemy who sought to hinder the building. Paul in Titus 1:9 carries out the thought of the symbol in this teaching that a bishop, a pastor, or a preacher, should be mighty in the holy Scriptures to instruct and admonish as well as to resist the gainsayers. Accordingly, we are to make a twofold use of the Word of God: as both bread and weapon; for feeding and for resisting; in peace and in war. With one hand we must build, improve, teach and feed all Christendom; with the other, oppose the devil, the heretics, the world. For where the pasture is not defended, the devil will soon destroy it; he is bitterly opposed to God's Word. Let us then, God granting us his grace, so handle the Gospel that not only shall the souls of men be fed, but men shall learn to put on that Gospel as armor and fight their enemies. Thus shall it furnish both pasture and weapons.

The first consideration in this lesson is, Paul teaches what should be the one theme of Titus and of every other preacher, namely, Christ. The people are to be taught who Christ is, why he came and what blessings his coming brought us. "The grace of God hath appeared," the apostle says, meaning God's grace is clearly manifest. How was it manifested? By the preaching of the apostles it was proclaimed worldwide. Previous to Christ's resurrection, the grace of God was unrevealed. Christ dwelt only among the Jews and was not yet glorified. But after his ascension he gave to men the Holy Spirit. Concerning the Spirit, he before testified (John 16:14) that the Spirit of truth, whom he should send, would glorify him.

The apostle's meaning is: Christ did not come to dwell on earth for his own advantage, but for our good. Therefore he did not retain his goodness and grace within himself. After his ascension he caused them to be proclaimed in public preaching throughout the world—to all men. Nor did he permit the revelation to be made as a mere proclamation of a fact, as a rumor or a report; it was appointed to bring forth fruit in us. It is a revelation and proclamation that teaches us to deny—to reject—ungodly things, all earthly lusts, all worldly desires, and thenceforward lead a sober, righteous and godly life.

In the first verse, the true essence of the text, "The grace of God hath appeared, bringing salvation to all men," Paul condemns the favors of the world and of men as pernicious, worthy of condemnation, ineffectual; and would incite in us a desire for divine grace. He teaches us to despise human favor. He who would have God's grace and favor must consider the surrender of all other grace and favor. Christ says (Matt. 10:22), "Ye shall be hated of all men for my name's sake." The Psalmist says (Ps. 53:5), "God hath scattered the bones of him that campeth against thee." And Paul declares (Gal. 1:10), "If I were still pleasing men, I should not be a servant of Christ." Where the saving grace of God comes, the pernicious favor of men must be ignored. He who would taste the former must reject and forget the latter.

According to the text, this grace has appeared, or is proclaimed, to all men. Christ commanded (Mark 16:15) that the Gospel be preached to all creatures throughout the whole world. And Paul in many places—for instance, Colossians 1:23—says, "The Gospel, which ye heard, was preached in all creation under heaven." The thought is, The Gospel was preached publicly in the hearing of all creatures, much more of all men. At first Christ preached the Gospel and only in the land of the Jews, knowledge of the Holy Scriptures being confined to that nation, as Psalm 76:2 and 147:19 declare. But afterward the Word was made free to all men; not confined to any particular section. Psalm 19:4 declares, "Their line is gone out through all the earth, and their words to the end of the world." This is spoken of the apostles.

But you may object,

> "Surely the words of the apostles did not, in their time, reach the end of the world; for nearly eight hundred years elapsed after the apostolic age before Germany was converted, and also recent discoveries show there are many islands and many countries where no indication of the grace of God appeared before the fifteenth century."

I reply: The apostle has reference to the character of the Gospel. It is a message calculated, from the nature of its inception and purpose, to go into all the world. At the time of the apostles it had already entered the greater and better part of the world. Up to that day, no message of like character was ever ordained. The Law of Moses was confined to the Jewish nation. Universal proclamation of the Gospel being for the most part accomplished at that time, and its completion being inevitable—as it is today—the Scripture phraseology makes it an accomplished fact.

In the Scriptures we frequently meet with what is called "synecdoche;" that is, a figure of speech whereby a part is made to stand for the whole. For instance, it is said that Christ was three days and three nights in the grave, when the fact is he passed one entire day, two nights, and portions of two other days in that place (Matt. 12:40). Again, we read (Matt. 23:37) of Jerusalem stoning the prophets, yet a large proportion of the inhabitants were godly people. Thus, too, the ecclesiastics are said to be avaricious, but among them are many righteous men. This way of speaking is common to all languages; especially is it found in the Holy Scriptures.

So the Gospel was in the apostolic day preached to all creatures; for it is a message introduced, designed and ordained to reach all creatures. To illustrate: A prince, having despatched from his residence a message and seeing it started upon the way, might say the message had gone to the appointed place even though it had not yet reached its destination. Similarly, God has sent forth his Gospel to all creatures even though it has not so far reached all. Note, the prophet says the voice of the apostles has "gone out through all the earth." He does not say their voice has reached the entire world, but is on the way—"is gone out." And so Paul means the Gospel is continuously preached and made manifest to all men. It is now on the way; the act is performed though the effect is not complete.

FIRST EVIL—UNGODLINESS

THE APPEARING OF grace, Paul says, instructs us in two things: one is described as "denying ungodliness and wordly lusts." We must explain these terms. The Latin word "impietas," which the apostle renders in the Greek "asebia" and which in Hebrew is "resa," I cannot find any one German word to express. I have made it "ungœttlich wesen," "ungodliness." The Latin and Greek terms do not fully convey the Hebrew meaning. "Resa," properly, is the sin of failing to honor God; that is, of not believing, trusting, fearing him, not surrendering to him, not submitting to his providence, not allowing him to be God. In this sin, those guilty of gross outward evils are deeply implicated indeed; but much more deeply involved are the wise, sainted, learned ecclesiasts who, relying upon their works, think themselves godly and so appear in the eyes of the world. In fact, all men who do not live a life committed to the pure goodness and grace of God are "impious," ungodly, even though they be holy enough to raise the dead, or perfect in continence and all other virtues. "Graceless" or "faithless" would seem to be the proper adjective to describe them. I shall, however, use the term "ungodly." Paul tells us that saving grace has appeared to the graceless to make them rich in grace and rich in God; in other words, to bring them to believe, trust, fear, honor, love and praise him, and thus transform ungodliness into godliness.

Of what use would be the appearing of saving grace were we to attempt to become godly in life through some other means? Paul here declares grace was revealed and proclaimed to the very end that we might deny ungodliness and thereafter live righteously; not through or of ourselves, but through grace. No one more disparages divine grace, and more gainsays its appearing, than do hypocrites and ungodly saints; for, unwilling to regard their own works ineffectual, sinful and faulty, they discover in themselves much good. Measuring themselves by their good intentions, they imagine they deserve great merit independently of grace. God, however, regards no work good—nor is it—unless he by his grace effects it in us. It was for the sake of accomplishing in us all many such works, and of deterring us from our own attempts, that God manifested his saving grace to men.

Now, the foremost evil of men is their godlessness, their unsaved state, their lack of grace. It includes first a faithless heart, and then all resultant thoughts, words, works and conduct in general. Left to himself, the individual's inner life and outward conduct are guided only by his natural abilities and human reason. In these his beauty and brilliance sometimes outshine the real saints. But he seeks merely his own interest. He is unable to honor God in life and conduct, even though he does command greater praise and glory in the exercise of reason than do the true saints of frequent Scripture mention. So worldwide and so deeply subtle an evil is this godless, graceless conduct, it withholds from the individual the power to perceive the evil of his way, to believe he errs, even when his error is held up to him. The prophet (Ps. 32:2) looks upon this blindness as not that of reason, or of the world, or of the flesh, but as a spiritual deception, leading astray not only the reason but the spirit of man.

In fact, that ungodliness is sinful must be believed rather than felt. Since God permitted the manifestation of his grace to all men to lead them to deny ungodliness, we ought to believe him a Being who knows our hearts better than we do ourselves. We must also confess that were it not for the ungodliness and faulty character of our deeds, God would not have ordained the proclamation of his grace for our betterment. Were one to administer remedies to an individual not ill, he would be looked upon as lacking sense. Accordingly, God must be regarded in the same light by them who, measuring themselves by their good intentions and their feelings, are unwilling to believe all their deeds ungodly and worthy of condemnation, and that God's saving grace is necessary. To them this is a terrible doctrine. Christ (Matt. 21:32) charges the chief priests, doctors and ecclesiasts (elders) with disbelieving John the Baptist, who called them to repentance; they refused to know their sin. All the prophets met death for accusing the people of the sin of ungodliness. No one believed the prophets. No one of the people thought himself guilty of such sin. They judged themselves by their feelings, their intentions and works; not by God's Word, not by his counsel delivered through the prophets.

Paul employs a strong Greek term, "pædeusa," meaning "to instruct"—such elementary instruction as we give children concerning a thing whereof they have no knowledge at all. The children are guided, not by their reason, but by the instructing word of their father. According to his representation they regard a certain thing as useful or as harmful. They believe in and are guided by him. With intelligent and learned individuals, however, we explain in a way comprehensible to their reason why a certain thing is profitable and a certain other thing unprofitable. God designs that we, as childish pupils, be instructed by his saving grace. Then if we cannot feel we may yet believe that our natures are godless and faulty, and so receive grace and walk therein. Well does Christ testify (Matt. 18:3), "Except ye turn, and become as little children, ye shall in no wise enter into the kingdom of heaven;" and Isaiah (7:9), "If ye will not believe, surely ye shall not be established." Divine, saving grace, then, has appeared, not only to help us, but also to teach us our need of grace. For the fact of its coming shows all our works godless, graceless, condemned. The psalmist (Ps. 119:5-8) fervently entreats God to teach him his judgments, laws and commandments, that he may not be guided by his own ideas and feelings, a thing God has forbidden (Deut. 12:8), saying: "Ye shall not do . . . every man whatsoever is right in his own eyes."

SECOND EVIL—WORLDLY LUSTS

THE OTHER EVIL in man Paul terms "worldly lusts." Therein is comprehended all disorderly conduct the individual may be guilty of, touching himself and his neighbor; while the first evil—ungodliness—comprehends all wrongs toward God. Observe Paul's judicious choice of words—"lusts," "worldly lusts." By the use of "worldly" he would include all evil lusts, whether it be for goods, luxuries, honor, favors or aught of the world wherein one may lustfully sin. He does not say, however, we must deny ourselves worldly goods, or must not make use of them. They are good creatures of God. We must avail ourselves of food, drink, clothing and other necessaries of life. No such thing is forbidden; it is only the lust after them, the undue love and craving for them, that we must deny, for it leads us into all sins against ourselves and our neighbors.

In this expression is also condemned the conduct of godless hypocrites, who, though they may be clad in sheep's clothing and sometimes refrain from an evil deed through cowardice or shame or through fear of hell's punishment, are nevertheless filled with evil desires for wealth, honor and power. No one loves life more dearly, fears death more terribly and desires more ardently to remain in this world than do they; yet they fail to recognize the worldly lusts wherein they are drowned, and their many works are vainly performed. It is not enough to put away wordly works and speech; worldly desires, or lusts, must be removed. We are not to place our affections upon the things of this life, but all our use of it should be with a view to the future life; as follows in the text: "Looking for the appearing of the glory," etc.

Observe here, the grace of God reveals the fact that all men are filled with worldly lusts, though some may conceal their lustfulness by their hypocrisy. Were men not subject to such desires, there could be no necessity for the revelation of grace, no need for its benefits, no occasion for its manifestation to all men, no need it should teach the putting off of lusts. For whosoever is not subject to lusts is not called upon to forsake them. Paul's statement here has no reference to such a one. Indeed, he cannot be a human being; hence he has no need of grace, and so far as he is concerned its manifestation is not essential. What, then, must he be? Unquestionably, a devil, and eternally condemned with all his holiness and purity. Could the hypocrites, however, wholly hide their worldly lusts, they could not conceal their ardent desire to hold to this life, and their unwillingness to die. Thus they reveal their lack of grace, and the worldliness and ungodliness of all their works. Nevertheless, they fail to perceive their graceless condition and their perilous infirmity.

Further, Paul speaks of "denying," or renouncing. Therein he rejects many foolish expedients devised by men for attaining righteousness. Some run to the wilderness, some into cloisters. Others separate themselves from society, presuming by bodily flight to run away from ungodliness and worldly lusts. Yet others resort to tortures and injuries of the body, imposing upon themselves excessive hunger, thirst, wakefulness, labor, uncomfortable apparel. Now, if ungodliness and worldly lusts were but something painted upon the wall, you might escape them by running out of the house; if they were knit into a red coat, you might pull off the coat and don a gray one; did they grow in your hair, you might have it shaved off and wear a bald pate; were they baked in the bread, you might eat roots instead. But since they inhere in your heart and permeate you through and through, where can you flee that you will not carry them with you? What can you wear under which you will escape them? What will you eat and drink wherein they will not be with you? In a word, what can you do to escape yourself, since you cannot get out of yourself? Dear man, the great temptations are within you. To run away from them would necessitate, first, fleeing from yourself. James says (1:14), "Each man is tempted, when he is driven away by his own lust, and enticed."

The apostle means, not simply that we must flee the outward temptations to sin, but, as he says, that we must "deny" them, must mortify the lusts, or desires, within ourselves. Our lusts being mortified, no external temptation can harm. By such subjection do we truly flee? If we fail to mortify our desires, it will not avail to flee outward temptations. We must remain amidst temptations and there learn through grace to deny lusts and ungodliness. It is written (Ps. 110:2), "Rule thou"—or apply thyself—"in the midst of thine enemies." Conflict and not flight, energy and not rest, must be the order in this life if we are to win the crown.

We read of an ancient father who, unable to endure temptation in a cloister, left it that he might in the wilderness serve God in peace. But in the desert one day his little water-jug overturned. He set it up, but it overturned a second time. Becoming enraged, he dashed the vessel into pieces. Then, saying within himself, "Since I cannot find peace when alone, the defect must be in myself," he returned to the cloister to suffer temptations, from that time forward teaching that we must obtain the victory, not by fleeing worldly lusts, but by denying them.

THE CHRISTIAN LIFE

PAUL GOES ON to show another thing wherein we are instructed of grace—the Christian's manner of life after ungodliness and worldly lusts are denied:

> **"We should live soberly and righteously and godly in this present world."**

What an excellent general rule of life he gives us! one adapted to all conditions. He offers no occasion for sects. He introduces no differing opinions of men, as the case is with human doctrines.

First, he mentions "soberness," wherein is indicated what should be the nature of man's conduct toward himself in all respects. It calls for the subjection of the body, the keeping of it well disciplined. In every place of our text where the term "soberness" is used, Paul has the Greek word "sophron," which signifies, not only soberness, but temperance in every recognition of the body, in every ministration to the flesh; in eating, drinking and sleeping, for instance; in apparel, speech, manner and movement. Such soberness represents what is known in German as honorable living and good breeding. The sober man knows how, in all physical relations, to conduct himself temperately, discreetly and bravely; not leading a wild, shameless, unrestrained, disorderly life, lax in regard to eating, drinking, sleeping, and to speech, manner and movement. In the earlier part of the chapter, Paul devises that aged women teach the young women to be "sober-minded" and chaste.

Excessive eating and drinking truly does greatly impede our efforts to lead an honorable life. On the other hand, temperance contributes much to accomplish it. The moment one indulges his appetite to excess, he loses perfect control of himself; his five senses become unmanageable. Experience teaches that when the stomach is filled with meat and drink, the mouth is filled with words, the ears with the lust of hearing, the eyes with the lust of seeing. The whole system either becomes indolent, drowsy, dull, or else it grows wild and dissolute, all the members overleaping the bounds of reason and propriety, until no discipline nor moderation remains. The word in our text, therefore, is not inaptly Latinized "sobrius," "soberness." In Greek, the word "sophron" is the opposite of "asotos," just as in German "vœllerei" and "mæszigkeit," "drunkenness" and "soberness," are contrasting terms. Examining the Latin "sobrius," we find it does not signify total abstinence from food and drink. "Sobrius" and "ebrius" are also contrasting terms, like the German "trunkenheit oder vœllerei" and "nuechterkeit," "drunkenness or ebriety" and "soberness." We Germans also call that individual "nuechtern," "sober," who, though he may have eaten and drunk, is not intoxicated, but has perfect control of himself.

You see now the manner of good works advocated by the apostle. He does not require us to make pilgrimages; he does not forbid certain foods; nor does he prescribe a particular garb, nor certain fast days. His teaching is not that of the class who, in obedience to human laws, separate themselves from men, basing their spirituality and goodness upon the peculiarity of their garb and diet, their manner of wearing the hair, their observance of times; who seek to become righteous by not conforming to custom in the matter of clothing, diet, occupation, seasons and movements. They are given an appropriate name in the Gospel—"pharisæi," meaning "excluded" or "separated." In Psalm 80:13, the prophet calls them "monios," signifying "a solitary one." The name primarily is applied to a wild hog of solitary habits. We shall hereafter designate this class as "solitary." As the psalmist complains, they make terrible havoc of God's vineyard. These Pharisees, or solitary ones, make great show with their traditions, their peculiar garb, their meats, days and physical attitudes. They easily draw away the multitude from the common customs of life to their ways. As Christ tells us (Matt. 24:24), even the elect can scarce resist them.

Let us learn here from Paul that no meats, drinks, apparel, colors, times, attitudes, are forbidden and none are prescribed. In all these things, everyone is given freedom, if only they be used in soberness, or moderation. As said before, these temporalities are not forbidden. Only the abuse of them, only excess and disorder therein, is prohibited. Where there is distinction and emphasis on such matters, there you will surely find human laws; not evangelical doctrine, not Christian liberty. Without soberness, or moderation, the ultimate result must be dissimulation, and hypocrisy. Therefore, make use of all earthly things when and where you please, giving thanks to God. This is Paul's teaching. Only guard against excess, disorder, misuse and licentiousness relative to temporal things and you will be in the right way. Do not permit yourself to be misled by the fact that the holy fathers established orders and sects, made use of certain meats and certain apparel, and conducted themselves thus and so. Their object was not peculiar eminence—therein they would have been unholy—but their conduct was of preference, and as a means for exercising moderation. Likewise do you exercise moderation as you see fit, and maintain your freedom. Confine not yourself to manners and methods, as if godly living consisted in them. Otherwise you will be solitary and deprived of the communion of saints. Diligently guard against such narrowness. We must fast, we must watch and labor, we must wear inferior clothing, and so on; but only on occasions when the body seems to need restraint and mortification. Do not set apart a specified time and place, but exercise your self-denial as necessity requires. Then you will be fasting rightly. You will fast every day in denying worldly lusts. So the Gospel teaches, and they who follow this course are of the New Testament dispensation.

Secondly, Paul says we should be "righteous" in our lives. No work, however, nor particular time, is here designated as the way to righteousness. In the ways of God is universal freedom. It is left to the individual to exercise his liberty; to do right when, where and to whom occasion offers. Herein Paul gives a hint of how we should conduct ourselves toward our neighbor—righteously. We owe him that righteousness which consists in doing to him as we would have him do to us; in granting to him all we would have him grant us. We are to do our neighbor no bodily harm, no injury to his wife, children, friends, possessions, honor or anything of his. Rather we are obligated, wherever we see he needs our assistance, to aid him, to stand by him, at the risk of our bodies, our property, our honor and everything that is ours. Righteousness consists in rendering to each one his due. What a little word to comprehend so much! How few walk in this way of righteousness, though otherwise living blamelessly! We do everything else but what saving grace reveals to us as our duty to do.

The word "neighbor" must be construed to include even an enemy. But the way of righteousness is entirely obliterated. It is much more overgrown in neglect than the way of moderation, which itself is almost wholly untrodden and effaced because of the introduction of certain meats and apparel, certain movements and display. These things have been superabundantly, more than profusely, insinuated. We ape after set forms, and make fools of ourselves with rosaries, with ecclesiastical and feudal institutions, with hearing of masses, with festivals, with self-devised works concerning which is no divine command. O Lord God, how wide hell has opened her mouth (see Isaiah 5:14); and how narrow has the gate of heaven become in consequence of the accursed doctrines and devices of these solitary and Pharisaical persons! The prophets unwittingly paint the picture of present-day conditions. They represent hell by the wide-open mouth of a dragon, and heaven by a closed door. Oh, the wretchedness of the picture!

It is not necessary to inquire what outward works you can perform. Look to your neighbor. There you will find enough to do, a thousand kind offices to render. Do not suffer yourself to be misled into believing you will reach heaven by praying and attending church, by contributing to institutions and monuments, while you pass by your neighbor. If you pass him in this life, he will lie in your way in the life to come and cause you to go by the door of heaven as did the rich man who left Lazarus lying at his gate. Wo to us priests, monks, bishops and Pope! What do we preach? What teach? How we lead the pitiable multitude from the way! The blind leading the blind, both shall fall into the ditch. Such doctrines as Paul declares in the conclusion of this lesson—these are what we should teach.

In the third place, we are taught we must live "godly" lives. Here we are reminded of how to conduct ourselves toward God. Now we are fully instructed concerning our duty to ourselves, to our neighbors and to God. As before said, impiety signifies wickedness, ungodliness, lack of grace. Piety, on the other hand, means having faith, godliness, grace. Godly living consists in trusting God, in relying on his grace alone, regarding no work not wrought in us by him, through grace. If we are godly, we will recognize, honor, adore, praise and love God. Briefly in two words, to live godly is to fear and trust God. As it is written (Ps. 147:11), "Jehovah taketh pleasure in them that fear him, in those that hope in his loving-kindness" (see also Ps. 33:18). To fear God is to look upon our own devices as pure ungodliness in the light of his manifest grace. These being ungodly, we are to fear God and forsake them, and thereafter guard against them. To trust in God is to have perfect confidence that he will be gracious to us, filling us with grace and godliness.

The individual yields to God when he gives himself wholly to God, attempting nothing of himself but permitting the Lord to work in and to rule him; when his whole concern and fear, his continual prayer and desire, are for God to withhold him from following his own works and ways, which he now recognizes as ungodly and deserving of wrath, and to rule over and work in him through grace. Thus the individual will obtain a clear conscience and will love and praise God. Observe, they are pious and filled with grace, who do not walk by reason, do not trust in human nature, but rely only on the grace of God, ever fearful lest they fall from grace into dependence upon their own reason, their self-conceit, good intentions and self-devised works. The theme of the entire one-hundred-and-nineteenth Psalm is trust in God. In every one of its one hundred and seventy-six verses, David breathes the same prayer. Reliance upon God is a subject of such vital importance, and so numerous are the difficulties and dangers attending human nature and reason and human doctrine, we cannot be too much on our guard.

The way of God does not require us to build churches and cathedrals, to make pilgrimages, to hear mass, and so on. God requires a heart moved by his grace, a life mistrustful of all ways not emanating from grace. Nothing more can one render God than such loyalty. All else is rather his gift to us. He says (Ps. 50:14-15), in effect: "Think not, O Israel, I inquire after thy gifts and offerings; for everything in heaven and earth is mine. This is the service I require of thee: to offer unto me thanksgiving and pay thy vows. Call upon me in the day of trouble and I will deliver thee, and thou shalt glorify me." In other words: Thou hast vowed that I should be thy God. Then keep this vow. Let me work; perform not thine own works. Let me help thee in thy need. For everything, look to me. Let me alone direct thy life. Then wilt thou be able to know me and my grace; to love and praise me. This is the true road to salvation. If thou doest otherwise, performing thine own works, thou wilt give thyself praise, wilt disregard me and refuse to accept me as thy God. Thou wilt prove treacherous and break thy vow.

Note, such obedience to God is real, divine service. For this service we need no bells nor churches, no vessels nor ornaments. Lights and candles are not necessary; neither are organs and singing, images and pictures, tables and altars. We require not bald pates nor caps, not incense nor sprinkling, not processions nor handling of the cross; neither are indulgences nor briefs essential. All these are human inventions, mere matters of taste. God does not regard them, and too often they obscure with their glitter the true service of God. Only one thing is necessary to right service—the Gospel. Let the Gospel be properly urged; through it let divine service be made known to the people. The Gospel is the true bell, the true organ, for divine service.

Further, Paul says we are to live as he describes "in this present world." First: the perfect life cannot be accomplished by works; our whole life, while we remain here, must be sober, righteous and godly. Christ promises (Matt. 10:22), "He that endureth to the end, the same shall be saved." Now, there are some who, it must be admitted, occasionally accomplish good; but occasional accomplishment is not a complete life of goodness, nor does it mean endurance to the end. Second: No one can afford to leave this matter of a godly life until death, or until another world is reached. Whatever we would have in the life to come must be secured here.

Many depend upon purgatory, living as it pleases them to the end and expecting to profit by vigils and soul masses after death. Truly, they will fail to receive profit therein. It were well had purgatory never been conceived of. Belief in purgatory suppresses much good, establishes many cloisters and monasteries and employs numerous priests and monks. It is a serious drawback to these three features of Christian living: soberness, righteousness and godliness. Moreover, God has not commanded, nor even mentioned, purgatory. The doctrine is wholly, or for the most part, deception; God pardon me if I am wrong. It is, to say the least, dangerous to accept, to build upon, anything not designated by God, when it is all we can do to stand in building upon the institutions of God which can never waver. The injunction of Paul to live rightly in this present world is truly a severe thrust at purgatory. He would not have us jeopardize our faith. Not that I, at this late day (when we write 1522), deny the existence of purgatory; but it is dangerous to preach it, whatever of truth there may be in the doctrine, because the Word of God, the Scriptures, make no mention of a purgatory.

Paul's chief reason, however, for making use of the phrase "in this present world" is to emphasize the power of God's saving grace. In the extreme wickedness of the world, the godly person is as one alone, unexampled as it were, a rose among thorns; therefore he must endure every form of misfortune, of censure, shame and wrong. The apostle's thought is: He who would live soberly, righteously and godly must expect to meet all manner of enmity and must take up the cross. He must not allow himself to be misled, even though he has to live alone, like Lot in Sodom and Abraham in Canaan, among none but the gluttonous, the drunken, the incontinent, unrighteous, false and ungodly. His environment is world and must remain world. He has to resist and overcome the enticements of earth, censuring worldly desires. To live right in this present world, mark you, is like living soberly in a saloon, chastely in a brothel, godly in a gaiety hall, uprightly in a den of murderers. The character of the world is such as to render our earthly life difficult and distressing, until we longingly cry out for death and the day of judgment, and await them with ardent desire; as the next clause in the text indicates. Life being subject to so many evils, its only hope is in being led by grace. Human nature and reason are at a loss to direct it.

"Looking for the blessed hope."

With these words the apostle makes the godly life clearly distinct from every other life. Here is the text that enables one to perceive how he measures up to the life of grace. Let all who presume to think they live godly, step forward and answer as to whether or no they delight in this hope, as here pictured; whether they are so prepared for the day of judgment that they await it with pleasure; whether they regard it as more than endurable, as even a blessed event to be contemplated with longing and with cheerful confidence. Is it not true that human nature ever shrinks from the judgment? Is it not true that if the advent of that day rested upon the world's pleasure in the matter, it would never come? And particularly in the case of hypocritical saints? Where, then, does human nature stand? Where reason? Where the free-will so much extolled as inclined to and potent for good? Why does free-will not only flee from good but shrink from that honor to the God of salvation which the apostle here refers to as a "blessed hope" and in which hope we shall be blessed? What is to prevent the conclusion here that they who shrink from the judgment lead lives impious, blamable and devoid of grace, the evils and ungodliness of which they might, but for the approach of that day, conceal? What is more ungodly than to strive against God's will? But is not that just what the individual does who would flee from the day wherein the honor of God shall be revealed, who does not await the event with a loving and joyful heart? Mark you, then, he who desires not that day and does not with delight and with love to God await it, is not living a godly life, not though he is able even to raise the dead.

"Then it must be," you say, "that few lead godly lives, particularly among those solitary, spiritual ones who above all men flee death and the judgment." That is just what I have said. These separated individuals simply lead themselves and others from the true path, obliterating the ways marked out of God. Plainly we see now how little reason and nature can accomplish; they but strive against God. And we see how necessary is saving grace. For when our own works are abandoned, God comes and alone works in us, enabling us to rise from ourselves, from our ungodly conduct, to a supernatural, grace-filled, godly life. Then we not only do not fear the day of judgment, but cheerfully, even longingly, await it, contemplating it with joy and pleasure. This point has been further treated in the Gospel lesson for the second Sunday in Advent.

True godliness, you note, is not taught by human nature or mortal reason, but by the manifest grace of God. By grace are we enabled to deny worldly lusts, even to feel aversion to them, to desire liberation from them, to be dissatisfied with our manner of life in general. More than that, it creates in us a disposition essential to godliness, a disposition to entreat God with perfect confidence and to await with pleasure his coming. So should we be disposed.

Now, let us carefully weigh the words "blessed hope." A contrast is presented to that miserably unhappy life wherein, when we attempt to walk uprightly, we are only harassed by misfortune, danger and sin. All in this life serves but to vex, while we have every reason to be encouraged in that hope. Such is the experience of them who earnestly endeavor to live soberly, righteously and godly. The world cannot long endure this class; it soon regards them as repulsive. Paul testifies (Rom. 5:3), "We also rejoice in our tribulations: knowing that tribulation worketh stedfastness; and stedfastness, approvedness; and approvedness, hope: and hope putteth not to shame." Thus our eyes remain closed to the wordly and visible, and open to the eternal and invisible. All this transformed condition is the work of grace, through the cross, which we must endure if we attempt to lead a godly life, the life the world cannot tolerate.

"And appearing of the glory."

Paul's word for "advent" here is "epiphaniam," "appearing" or "manifestation." Similarly, he spoke above of the "appearance" or "manifestation" of grace. The word "advent" in the Latin, therefore, does not express all. The apostle would make a distinction between the first appearing and the last. The first appearing was attended by humility and dishonor, with intent to attract little attention and occasion no manifestation but that made in faith and through the Gospel. Christ is at present not manifest in person, but on the day of judgment he will appear in effulgent splendor, in undimmed honor; a splendor and honor eternally manifest to all creatures. The last day will be an eternal day. Upon the instant of its appearing every heart and all things will stand revealed. Such is the meaning of "the appearing of glory" mentioned, the appearance of Christ's honor. Then there will be neither preaching nor faith. To all men everything will be manifest by experience, and by sight as in a clear-day. Hence Paul adds,

"Of the great God and our Saviour Jesus Christ."

Not that another and lesser God exists; but that God has reserved unto the last day the displaying of his greatness and majesty, his glory and effulgence. We behold him now in the Gospel and in faith—a narrow view of him. Here he is not great because but slightly comprehended. But in the last appearing he will permit us to behold him in his greatness and majesty.

The words of this verse afford comfort to all who live soberly, righteously and godly. For the apostle therein declares the coming glory, not of our enemy or judge, but of our Saviour, Jesus Christ, who will at that time give us perfect happiness. For the day of that glorious appearing he will make the occasion of our liberation from this world wherein we must endure so much in the effort to lead a godly life in response to his will. In view of his coming and our great and glorious redemption, we ought firmly and cheerfully to bear up under the persecution, murders, shame and misfortunes the world effects, and to be courageous in the midst of death. With these joys before us, we ought the more steadfastly to persevere in a godly life, boldly relying upon the Saviour, Jesus Christ.

On the other hand, the words of this verse are terrible to the worldly-minded and wicked who are unwilling to endure, for the sake of godliness, the persecutions of the world. They prefer to make their godliness go no farther than to live without friction in the world and thus avoid incurring enmity and trouble. But the dissolute, the reckless, the obdurate, utterly disregard those words. They never give a thought to the fact of having to appear on the final day. Like frenzied animals, they run blindly and heedlessly on to the day of judgment and into the abyss of hell. You may ask, "How shall I obtain the godliness fitted to enable me to confidently await that day, since human nature and reason flee from a godly life and cannot accomplish it?" Observe what follows,

"Who gave himself for us."

The things the apostle has been so carefully presenting are laid before you to enable you to perceive and acknowledge your helplessness, to utterly despair of your own power, that you may sincerely humble yourself and recognize your vanity, and your ungodliness, impiety and unsaved state. Note, the grace appearing through the Gospel teaches humility; and being humbled, one desires grace and is disposed to seek salvation. Wherever a humble desire for grace exists, there is open to you the door of grace. The desire cannot be without provision for its fulfilment. Peter says (1 Pet. 5:5), "God resisteth the proud, but giveth grace to the humble." And Christ frequently in the Gospel declares: "Whosoever shall exalt himself shall be humbled; and whosoever shall humble himself shall be exalted."

So the blessed Gospel is presented to you. It permits saving grace to appear in and shine forth from you, teaching you what more is required to keep you from falling into despair. Now, the Gospel, the appearance of the light of grace, is this which the apostle here declares, namely, that Christ gave himself for us, etc. Therefore, hearken to the Gospel; open the windows of your heart and let saving grace shine forth, to enlighten and teach you. This truth, that Christ gave himself for us, is the message spoken of as proclaimed to all men. It is the explanation of what is meant by the appearing of grace.

Banish from your mind, then, the error into which you may have fallen, of thinking that to hear the epistles of Paul and Peter is not to hear the Gospel. Do not allow yourself to be misled by the name "epistle." All Paul writes in his epistles is pure Gospel. He says so in Romans 1:1 and in 1 Corinthians 4:15. In fact, I venture to say the Gospel is more vividly presented in the epistles of Paul than in the four books of the evangelists. The latter detail the life and words of Christ, which were understood only after the advent of the Holy Spirit, who glorified Christ. Thus the Saviour himself testifies. Paul, though he records no account of the life of Christ, clearly explains the purpose of our Lord's coming, and shows what blessings his advent brings to us. What else is the Gospel but the message that Christ gave himself for us, to redeem us from sin, and that all who believe it will surely be saved?

So we are to despair of our own efforts and cleave to Christ, relying upon him alone. Gracious, indeed, and comforting is this message, and readily welcomed by hearts despairing of their own efforts. "Evangelium," or Gospel, implies a loving, kind, gracious message, fitted to gladden and cheer a sorrowing and terrified heart.

Take heed to believe true what the apostle, through the Gospel, declares—that Christ gave himself for you for the sake of redeeming you from all unrighteousness and of purifying you for a peculiar inheritance. It follows that, in the first place, you must believe and confess all your efforts, impure, unrighteous; and that your human nature, reason, art and free-will are ineffectual apart from Christ. Unless you so believe, you make void the Gospel; for, according to the Gospel, Christ did not give himself for the righteous and the pure. Why should he? With righteousness and purity existent, he would be giving himself in vain. It would be a senseless giving.

In the second place, you must believe that Christ gave himself for you, to put away your impurity and unrighteousness and make you pure and righteous in himself. If you believe this, it will be so. Faith will accomplish it. The fact that he gave himself for you can make you pure and righteous only through faith on your part. Peter (Acts 15:9) speaks of the cleansing of hearts by faith. Observe, Christ is not put into your hand, not given you in a coffer, not placed in your bosom nor in your mouth. He is presented to you through the Word, the Gospel; he is held up before your heart, through the ears he is offered to you, as the Being who gave himself for you—for your unrighteousness and impurity. Only with your heart can you receive him. And your heart receives when it responds to your opened mind, saying, "Yes, I believe." Thus through the medium of the Gospel Christ penetrates your heart by way of your hearing, and dwells there by your faith. Then are you pure and righteous; not by your own efforts, but in consequence of the guest received into your heart through faith. How rich and precious these blessings!

Now, when faith dwelling within you brings Christ into your heart, you cannot think him poor and destitute. He brings his own life, his Spirit—all he is and commands. Paul says the Spirit is given, not in response to any work of man, but for the sake of the Gospel. The Gospel brings Christ, and Christ brings the Spirit—his Spirit. Then the individual is made new; he is godly. Then all his deeds are well wrought. He is not idle; for faith is never inactive. It continually, in word and act, proclaims Christ. Thus the world is roused against Christ; it will not hear, will not tolerate, him. The result is crosses for the Christian, and crosses render life loathsome and the day of judgment desirable. This, mark you, explains the Gospel and the appearing of the saving grace of God.

How can death and the day of judgment terrify the heart that receives Christ? Who shall injure such a one when the great God and Saviour, Jesus Christ, who orders the day of judgment, stands by with all his glory, greatness, majesty and might? He who gave himself for us, he and no other, will control that day. Assuredly he will not deny his own testimony, but will verify your faith by declaring he gave himself for your sins. And what have you to fear from sin when the judge himself owns he has taken it away by his own sacrifice? Who will accuse you? Who may judge the Judge? Who exercise authority over him?

His power outweighs that of all the world with its sins innumerable. Had he purchased your salvation with anything but himself, there might be great error in this doctrine. But what can terrify when he has given himself for you? He would have to condemn himself before sin could condemn the souls for whom he died.

Here is strong, unquestionable security. But our connection with it depends upon the steadfastness of our faith. Christ certainly will not waver. He is absolutely steadfast. We should, then, urge and enforce faith by our preaching and in our working and suffering, ever making it firm and constant. Works avail nothing here. The evil spirit will assail only our faith, well knowing that upon it depends all. How unfortunate our failure to perceive our advantage! for we ignore the Gospel with its saving grace. Wo unto you, Pope, bishops, priests and monks! Of what use are you in the churches and occupying the pulpits? Now let us analyze the words,

"That he might redeem us."

He gave himself to redeem—not himself, but us. Evidently, we are naturally captives. Then how can we be presumptuous and ungrateful enough to attribute so much merit to our free-will and our natural reason? If we claim there is aught in us not bound in sin, we disparage the grace whereby, according to the Gospel, we are redeemed. Who can do any good thing while captive in sin, while wholly unrighteous? Our own efforts may seem to us good, but in truth they are not; otherwise, the Gospel of Christ must be false.

"From all iniquity."

The word Paul uses for "iniquity" is "anomias," the specific meaning of which is, anything not conforming to the Law, whether transgression of soul or body, the former transgression being ungodliness or impiety, and the latter worldly lusts. He is careful to add the word "all," to make plain the inclusion of the sins of the body and the unrighteousness of soul wherefrom Christ has completely redeemed us. This teaching is a blow at the self-righteous and separate, who redeem themselves, and others as well, from certain forms of unrighteousness by means of the Law, or by their own reason and free-will. In reality they do avoid the outward act of transgression, being restrained by prohibitions, or fear of pain and penalty, or expectation of reward or gain. But this is only ridding of the scum of unrighteousness; the heart remains filled with ungodly, unregenerate inclination and worldly lusts, and neither body nor soul is righteous. But through faith Christ redeems us from all unrighteousness. He liberates us, enabling us to live godly and heavenly, a power we had not when in the prison of unrighteousness.

"And purify unto himself."

Sin is attended by two evils: First, it takes us captive. In its power we are incapable of doing good, of desiring or even recognizing good. Sin thus robs us of power, freedom and light. The second evil attendant upon sin is the natural outcome of the first: we forsake good to engage only in iniquity and impurity, tilling with hard and heavy labor the land of wicked Pharaoh in Egypt. But when, through faith, Christ comes, he liberates from the bondage of Egypt and gives power to do good. That power is our first gain.

Afterward, the effort of our entire lives should be to purge from body and soul unrighteous, unregenerate, and worldly conduct. Until death our lives should be nothing but purification. While it is true that faith instantly redeems from all legal guilt and sets free, yet evil desires remain in body and soul, as odor and disease cling to a dungeon. Faith occupies itself with purifying from these. Typical of this principle, Lazarus in the Gospel was raised from the dead by a single word (John 11:44), but afterward the shroud and napkin had to be removed. And the half-dead man whose wounds the Samaritan bound up and whom the Samaritan carried home, had to remain in the inn until he was restored.

"A people for his own possession."

The thought is of ownership—a peculiar inheritance or possession. The Scriptures term God's people his inheritance. As a landholder cultivates, nourishes and improves his inheritance, so, through the medium of our faith, Christ, whose inheritance we are, cultivates us, or impels us to daily grow better and more fruitful. Thus you see, faith liberates from sin, but more than that, it makes us Christ's inheritance, which he accepts and protects as his own. Who can injure us when we are the inheritance of the mighty God?

"Zealous of good works."

As ungodliness is opposed by inheritance, so zeal or diligence in our efforts after good opposes worldly lusts. By inward godliness we become Christ's heritage, and by sober and righteous living are good works wrought. As his heritage we serve him, and by good works we serve our neighbors and ourselves; first the heritage, then the good works. For good works are not wrought without godliness, and we are taught we must be zealous—zelotæ—that is, must emulate one another in doing good, or vie with one another in the effort to work universal good, disputing who was the best and who did the most good. This is the real meaning of the word "zelotæ." Where are these now?

"These things speak and exhort."

Truly, O Lord God, it is a vital charge, this—not only to preach the principles taught in this lesson, but continually to urge, admonish and arouse the people, leading them to faith and actually good works. Though we may have taught, we must follow it up with persevering exhortation, that the Word of God may have its sway.

O Pope, bishops, priests and monks now flooding the Church with fables and human doctrines, let these things sink into your minds. You will have more than enough to preach if you attempt only what this text contains, provided you continually admonish the people and enforce it. It beautifully portrays the life of the Christian. Its teaching, and only this, are you to preach and enforce. God grant it! Amen.

Note, the office of a minister calls for two things—teaching and exhortation. We must teach the uninformed, and must admonish the already informed lest they go backward, grow indolent or fall away entirely instead of persevering against all temptations.

THE ARMOR FURNISHED BY THE TEXT

FIRST, THE TEXT gives us authority to maintain that without grace no good can be wrought and all human efforts are sinful. This principle is established by Paul's statement, "Grace hath appeared." Evidently, previous to the advent mentioned, no grace existed among men. If no grace existed, plainly there was only wrath. Therefore, without grace, there is in ourselves nothing but unregeneracy and wrath, instead of good.

Again, Paul's reference to saving grace clearly indicates that whatever is devoid of grace is already condemned and beyond the power of procuring help and salvation. Where, then, is free will? Where are human virtues, human reason and opinions? All are without saving grace, all are condemned, sinful and shameful before God, even though precious in our sight.

Still more impressive is the phrase "to all men." None are excepted. Manifestly, then, until recognition of the Gospel, naught but wrath ruled in all men. The apostle says (Eph. 2:3), "We were by nature children of wrath, even as the rest." Here he repels with safe armor, and stops the mouths of, all who boast of reason, works, opinions, free-will, light of nature, etc., as efficacious without grace. He makes them all corrupt, impious, ungodly and devoid of grace.

Further, Paul declares the grace of God appeared to "all men" to enable them to "deny ungodliness and worldly lusts." Who can stand before the armor he uses? What is the inevitable conclusion but this: without the grace of God, the works of all men are ungodliness and worldly lusts? For were there godliness, or spiritual aspirations, in any individual, there would be no reason for "all men" to deny ungodliness and worldly lusts; neither would the saving appearance of grace be called for in all cases. In this way, mark you, we should use the Scriptures as armor against false teachers. Not only are they for the exercise of our faith in our daily living, but for the open defense and battle of faith against the attacks of error.

Before the testimony of this text, all hypocrites, all ecclesiastics, must lie prostrate in defeat, no matter how much they may have fasted, prayed, watched and toiled. These exertions will avail naught; ungodliness and worldly lusts will still survive in them. Though shame may cause them to conceal evil expression, the heart is still impure.

Could our works, apparel, cloisters, fasting and prayers render us godly, the apostle might more properly have said that a prayer or a fast, a pilgrimage or an order, or something else, had appeared teaching us to be godly. But emphatically it is none of these; it is the appearing of saving grace. This, this alone, nothing else, renders us godly.

The danger and error of human laws, orders, sects, vows, and so on, is easily apparent. For they are not grace; they are merely works, by their false appearance leading the whole world into error, distress and misery. Under their influence, the world forgets grace and faith, and looks for godliness and happiness in these errors.

Again, Paul's admonition to us to look for the blessed and glorious appearing of the great God establishes the fact of another life beyond this. Plainly, it is evident that the soul is immortal; yes, that even the body must rise again. We say in the creed, "I believe in the resurrection of the body and in the life everlasting."

Further, it may be logically inferred from Paul's language—"the great God and our Saviour Jesus Christ"—that Christ is true God. Clearly, then, it follows that the Being to come in glory on the judgment day is the great God and our Saviour, Jesus Christ.

Should one in a caviling spirit apply to the Father alone the reference here to "the great God," his theory would not hold. For this glorious appearing is shared by the great God and our Saviour, Jesus Christ. Were Christ not true God, the glory and splendor of God would not be attributed to him. Since mention is made of the splendor, the glory, the work, of "the great God and our Saviour" the latter must be God with the former. Through the mouth of Isaiah, God has more than once said, "My glory will I not give to another," and yet here he shares it with Christ. Hence Christ can be no other than God. The glory of God is his. Yet he is a person distinct from the Father.

Once more, a strong argument against human doctrine is afforded us in Paul's words, "These things speak and exhort." Had Paul designed anything further to be taught than the things he mentions, he surely would have said so. Our bishops and popes today think they have done enough when they permit these Paul's injunctions to be written in books and on slips of paper, enforcing them by no commands of their own; but the fact is, their own voices should be heard in constant preaching and enforcing of the Gospel. Wo unto them!

6

Second Christmas Sermon

(Early Christmas Morning Service)

"But when the kindness of God our Saviour, and his love toward man, appeared, not by works done in righteousness, which we did ourselves, but according to his mercy he saved us, through the washing of regeneration and renewing of the Holy Spirit, which he poured out upon us richly, through Jesus Christ our Saviour; that, being justified by his grace, we might be made heirs according to the hope of eternal life. Faithful is the saying, and concerning these things I desire that thou affirm confidently, to the end that they who have believed God may be careful to maintain good works. These things are good and profitable unto men" (Titus 3:4-8).

GOD'S GRACE RECEIVED MUST BE BESTOWED

THIS EPISTLE SELECTION inculcates the same principle taught in the conclusion of the Gospel lesson pertaining to contentment, good will and love for our neighbor. The substance of the text is: Why should we be unwilling to do for others what has been done for us by God, of whose blessings we are far less worthy than anyone can be of our help? Since God has been friendly and kindly disposed toward us in bestowing upon us his loving kindness, let us conduct ourselves similarly toward our neighbors, even if they are unworthy, for we too are unworthy.

It is necessary to a ready understanding of this epistle that we know the occasion of these words. In the verses immediately preceding, Paul says to Titus, his disciple:

"Put them in mind to be in subjection to rulers, to authorities, to be obedient, to be ready unto every good work, to speak evil of no man, not to be contentious, to be gentle, showing all meekness toward all men. For we also once were foolish, disobedient, deceived, serving divers lusts and pleasures, living in malice and envy, hateful, hating one another."

Note that Paul here indicates the relation we sustain to God and man. He would have us obedient to magistrates and kind to neighbors. Though our neighbors may be blind, erring and wicked, yet we should be charitable in our judgment and cheerfully endeavor to please them, remembering God's similar attitude toward us when we were as they.

The word "appeared," implying the revelation of the Gospel, or Christ's appearance to the whole world, is sufficiently defined in the preceding epistle lesson. Though in that case it refers to the birth of Christ, little depends on the circumstance so far as the meaning of the word is concerned. Paul does not employ here the little word "grace" used there, but he described the God of grace with two other pleasing words—"kindness" and "love." The first is, in Greek, "Chrestotes" (friendliness), implying that friendly, lovable demeanor which makes the individual attractive and gives his society a gracious influence moving everyone within its circle to love and affection. Such a one is capable of bearing with all men. He is not inclined to neglect any nor to repel with harshness. In him everyone may repose confidence. All men can approach him and deal with him. He resembles Christ, whom the Gospel portrays as always friendly to everyone, repelling none but gracious unto all.

God, too, shows himself to us through the Gospel as wholly lovable and kind, receiving all, rejecting none, ignoring our shortcomings and repelling no soul by severity. The Gospel proclaims naught but grace, whereby God sustains us and through which he kindly leads us, regardless of our worthiness. This is the day of grace. All men may confidently draw near to the throne of his mercy, as it is written in Hebrews 4:16. And we read in Psalm 34:5, "They looked unto him, and were radiant; and their faces shall never be confounded." That is, God will not permit us to ask in vain, or to come unto him and go away empty and ashamed.

The second Word is, in Greek, "Philanthropia" (Philanthropy)—love of mankind. Avarice is the love of money. David (2 Sam. 1:26) refers to "the love of women." But naturalists term certain animals—the dog, the horse, the dolphin—philanthropic or humane, because they have a natural love and fondness for man; they adapt themselves to his service as if endowed with reason enabling them to understand him.

It is an attitude of love for mankind the apostle here attributes to our God. Moses has done likewise in Deuteronomy 33:2-3, where he says of God: "At his right hand was a fiery law for them. Yea, he loveth the people." This quotation indicates that God does more than show himself, through the Gospel, with a kindly bearing, desiring to draw men unto himself, and tolerant of their shortcomings; he would give them of himself, would bestow his presence, and he extends his grace and friendship.

These two words descriptive of God, "kindness" and "love," are indeed pleasant and consoling. They represent him as offering grace, following us, ready to receive most graciously all who draw near to him and desire him. What more could he do? Note now why the Gospel is termed a gracious, comforting message concerning God revealed in Christ. What can be conceived more gracious to a poor, sinful conscience than what these words convey? Oh, how wretchedly the devil, through the laws of the Pope, has perverted for us these pure words of God!

These two words are to be accepted with their full and broad import. No distinction of person, as prevails among men, is to be made: for divine love and kindness is not secured by human merit; it is of God's grace alone and given to all that bear the name of man, however insignificant. God loves not what is characteristic of one person, but of all. He is partial not to one, but kind to all. Therefore a man's honor is perfectly maintained, and no one can boast of his worthiness, or need despair because of his unworthiness. All mankind may be equally comforted in the unmerited grace God kindly and humanely offers and applies.

Had there ever been a meritorious individual or a work worthy of consideration, it surely would have been found among the doers of "works of righteousness." But Paul rejects especially these, saying, "not by works of righteousness which we have done." How much less reason have we to think the kindness and love of God has appeared in consequence of man's wisdom, power, nobility, wealth and the color of his hair! The grace which cancels all our boasted honor, ascribing glory alone to God who freely bestows it upon the unworthy, is pure as well as great.

This epistle instills the two further principles of believing and loving—receiving favors from God and granting favors to our neighbors. The entire Scriptures enforce these two precepts, and the practice of one requires the practice of the other. He who does not firmly believe in God's grace assuredly will not extend kindness to his neighbor, but will be tardy and indifferent in aiding him. In proportion to the strength of his faith will be his willingness and industry in helping his neighbor. Thus faith incites love, and love increases faith.

Now we see how utterly we fail to walk in faith when we presume to arrive at goodness and happiness by any other good works than those done to our neighbor. So numerous are the new works and doctrines daily devised, everything like a correct conception of a truly good life is wholly destroyed. But the fact is, all Christian doctrines and works, all Christian living, is briefly, clearly and completely comprehended in these two principles, faith and love. They place man as a medium between God and his neighbor, to receive from above and distribute below. Thus the Christian becomes a vessel, or rather a channel, through which the fountain of divine blessings continuously flows to other individuals.

Mark you, the truly godlike are they who receive from God all he offers through Christ, and in return accredit themselves by their beneficence, performing for others the part God performs for them. Psalm 82:6 is in point here: "I said, Ye are gods, and all of you sons of the Most High." Sons of God are we, through the faith that constitutes us heirs of all divine blessings. But we are also "gods" through the love that makes us beneficent toward our neighbor. The divine nature is simply pure beneficence, or as Paul here says, kindness and love, daily pouring out blessings in abundance upon all creatures; as we everywhere witness.

Take heed, then, to embrace the message of these words presenting the love and kindness of God to all men. Daily exercise your faith therein, entertaining no doubt of God's love and kindness toward you, and you shall realize his blessings. Then you may with perfect confidence ask what you will, what your heart desires, and whatever is necessary for the good of yourself and your fellow-men. But if you do not so believe, it were far better you had never heard the message. For by unbelief you make false these precious, comforting, gracious words. You conduct yourself as if you regarded them untrue, which attitude is extreme dishonor to God; no more enormous sin could be committed.

But if you possess faith, your heart cannot do otherwise than laugh for joy in God, and grow free, confident and courageous. For how can the heart remain sorrowful and dejected when it entertains no doubt of God's kindness to it, and of his attitude as a good friend with whom it may unreservedly and freely enjoy all things? Such joy and pleasure must follow faith; if they are not ours, certainly something is wrong with our faith. This act of faith the apostle in Galatians terms "receiving the Holy Spirit" in and through the Gospel. The Gospel is a message concerning the love and mercy of God so gracious as to bring with it to preacher and hearer the presence of the Holy Spirit; just as the rays of the sun bear in themselves, and transmit, heat.

How could Paul have presented words conveying more love and graciousness? I venture to assert I have never read, in the entire Scriptures, words more beautifully expressive of the grace of God than these two—"Chrestotes" and "Philanthropia," friendliness and philanthropy. They represent grace not only as procuring for us remission of sins, but as God ever present with us, embracing us in his friendship, ever ready to help us and offering to do for us according to all we desire; in short, as a good and willing friend, to whom we may look for every favor and accommodation. Picture to your imagination a sincere friend and you will have an idea of God's attitude toward you in the person of Christ, though a very imperfect representation of his superabundant grace.

Now, if you steadfastly believe, if you rejoice in God your Lord, if you are alive and his grace satisfies, if your wants are all supplied, how will you employ yourself in this earthly life? Inactive you cannot be. Such a disposition of love toward God cannot rest. Your zeal will be warm to do everything you know will be to the praise and glory of a kind and gracious God. At this point there is no longer distinction of works. Here all commands terminate. There is neither restraint nor compulsion, but a joyful willingness and delight in doing good, whether the intended achievement be insignificant or difficult, small or great, requiring short service or long.

Your first desire will be that all men may obtain the same knowledge of divine grace. Hence your love will not be restrained from serving all to the fullest extent, preaching and proclaiming the divine truth wherever possible, and rejecting all doctrine and life not in harmony with this teaching. But take note, the devil and the world, unwilling that their devices be rejected, cannot endure the knowledge of what you do. They will oppose you with everything great, learned, wealthy and powerful, and represent you as a heretic and insane.

Mark you, you will be brought to the cross for the sake of the truth, as was Christ your Lord. You will have to endure the extremity of reproach. You must endanger all your property, friends and honor, your body and life, until thrust out of this life into eternity. In the midst of these trials, however, rejoice, cheerfully enduring all. Regard your enemies with the utmost charity. Act kindly, ever remembering you yourself were once as they are in the sight of God. Faith and love certainly can do it. Note this: the truly Christian life is that which does for others as God has done for itself.

Such is the apostle's meaning when he tells us the kindness of God did not appear unto us, or save us, because of our righteousness. His thought is: If we, though unworthy, were received through mercy, to enjoy the favors of God in spite of our great demerits and the enormity of our sins, why should we withhold our favors from others, whose merits have claims upon us? Let us not withhold; no, let us rather be children of God, doing good even to our enemies and to evil-doers: for so God has done, and still does, to us, evil-doers and his enemies. This teaching is in harmony with Christ's (Matt. 5:44-46),

> "Love your enemies . . . that ye may be sons of your Father who is in heaven; for he maketh his sun to rise on the evil and the good, and sendeth rain on the just and the unjust. For if ye love them that love you, what reward have ye? do not even the publicans the same?"

Paul not only forcibly rejects us for our evil deeds, but goes so far as to say, "Not by works of righteousness which we have done." He means the works regarded by ourselves as good—our righteousness in our own eyes and in the eyes of others—but which only render us more unfit to receive God's grace because they are in themselves deceitful and because we commit a twofold sin in looking upon them as good and in relying upon them; an attitude to provoke God's displeasure.

Similarly do our enemies, who while in the wrong yet maintain, in opposition to us, their faultlessness, for the most part provoke us to anger. Yet we are not to refuse them kindness. God, solely for his mercy's sake, refused not kindness to us in similar errors, when we foolishly imagined all we did was right. As he dealt not with us according to our imagined righteousness, so should we in return not deal with our enemies according to their merits or demerits, but assist them from pure love, looking for thanks and reward, not from them, but from God. Let this be sufficient for a summary of this epistle.

Now let us consider the words Paul employs to define and advocate grace. In the first place he exalts it to the rejection of all our righteousness and good works. We are not to conclude it is a trivial thing he is rejecting here. It is man's best earthly achievement—righteousness. Were all men to concentrate their united efforts to attain wisdom and virtue by their natural reason, knowledge and free will—as we read, for instance, of the illustrious virtues and wisdom of certain pagan teachers and princes, Socrates, Trajan, and others, to whom all the world gives written and oral applause—were all men so to do, yet such wisdom and virtue are, in the sight of God, nothing but sin, and altogether reprehensible. The reason is, they are not attained in the grace of God; the achievers know not God and have not honored him in the effort, for they consider they have wrought by their own abilities. Righteousness is not taught otherwise than by grace, in the Gospel.

Paul boasts that he once led a life altogether irreproachable, and superior to the lives of his intellectual equals (Gal. 1:14), wherein he presumptuously thought he did right in persecuting the Christians who rejected that sort of piety. But after he had learned to know Christ, he declared he regarded his righteousness but filth and refuse that he might be found, not in his own righteousness, but in Christ and in faith, as he further shows in Philippians 3:9 and Galatians 1:14.

So he discards all boasted free will, all human virtue, righteousness and good works. He concludes they all are nothing and are wholly perverted, however brilliant and worthy they may appear, and teaches that we must be saved solely by the grace of God, which is effective for all believers who desire it from a correct conception of their own ruin and nothingness.

Now, it is essential that we accustom ourselves to interpret rightly the Scripture teaching of two kinds of righteousness. There is a human righteousness, to which Paul here and often elsewhere refers, and a divine righteousness—or divine grace—which justifies us through faith. Paul so expresses it in the conclusion of this epistle: "That, being justified by his grace, we might be made heirs according to the hope of eternal life." You see, the grace of God, and righteousness, become ours; we say "righteousness of God" because he gives it, and "our righteousness" because we receive it.

In Romans 1:17 Paul tells us that the Gospel declares the righteousness of God is obtained through faith; "as it is written, The righteous shall live by faith." And it is stated of Abraham in Genesis 15:6, "And he believed in Jehovah; and he reckoned it to him for righteousness." So the Scripture conclusion is, no one is justified before God except the believer; witness the quotation just given and that other by Paul from Habakkuk 2:4, "The righteous shall live by his faith." So faith, grace, mercy and truth are one thing, wrought in us by God, through the Gospel of Christ; as it is written, "All the paths of Jehovah are loving-kindness and truth" (Ps. 25:10).

We walk in "the paths of Jehovah," and he is in us when we observe his commandments. To be God's, the way must proceed in divine mercy and truth; not in our own ability or strength, for such are, in the eyes of God, ways of wrath and falsehood. He says (Is. 55:9), "For as the heavens are higher than the earth, so are my ways higher than your ways." In other words, "Your ways are earthly and ineffectual; you must walk in my heavenly ways if you are to be saved."

"But according to his mercy he saved us."

How are these words, reading as if we were already saved, to pass criticism? Are we not still on earth, in the midst of afflictions? I answer: The statement is made in just this way to emphasize the power of divine grace and the character of faith as opposed to the erring self-righteous, who essay to obtain salvation through their works, as if it were not right at hand. But salvation is not so to be attained. Christ has saved us once for all, and in a twofold manner: First, he has done all that is necessary for our salvation—conquered and destroyed sin, death and hell, leaving no more there for anyone to do. Secondly, he has conveyed all these blessings unto us in baptism. He who confidently believes Christ has accomplished these things, immediately, in the twinkling of an eye, possesses salvation. All his sins and the reality of death and hell are removed. Nothing more than such faith is necessary to salvation.

Take note, God pours out upon us in baptism superabundant blessings for the purpose of excluding the works whereby men foolishly presume to merit heaven and gain happiness. Yes, dear friend, you must first possess heaven and salvation before you can do good works. Works never merit heaven; heaven is conferred purely of grace. Good works are to be performed without any thought of merit, simply for the benefit of one's neighbor and for the honor of God; until the body, too, shall be released from sin, death and hell. The true Christian's whole life after baptism is but a waiting for the manifestation of the salvation already his. He is certainly in full possession of the eternal life yet concealed in faith.

When faith is removed by fulfilment, salvation is manifest in the believer. This takes place at physical death. It is written (1 John 3:2-3),

> "Beloved, now are we children of God, and it is not yet made manifest what we shall be. We know that, if he shall be manifested, we shall be like him; for we shall see him even as he is. And every one that hath this hope set on him purifieth himself, even as he is pure."

Therefore, let not the work-righteous who disregard faith mislead you, placing your salvation far ahead of you and compelling you to obtain it by works. It is within you, dear friend; it is already obtained. Christ says (Luke 17:21), "The kingdom of God is within you." Hence the life we live after baptism is but a tarrying, a waiting and longing for the manifestation of what is within ourselves, an apprehension of that for which we are apprehended. Paul declares (Phil. 3:12), "I follow after, if that I may apprehend that for which also I am apprehended of Christ Jesus"; that is, that he may see the blessings given in the shrine of faith. The apostle is eager to behold the treasure that baptism has granted and sealed to him in faith.

In this same third chapter of Philippians Paul says, "Our citizenship is in heaven"—that is, now—"whence also we wait for a Saviour, the Lord Jesus Christ: who shall fashion anew the body of our humiliation, that it may be conformed to the body of his glory." In Galatians 4:9, when saying, "Now that ye have come to know God," he recalls the words and adds, "or rather to be known by God." While both these things are in point, there is a difference in their meaning: we are known of God, already apprehended; but we do not yet know and apprehend him. Our knowledge is hidden and withholden in faith.

Again, the apostle tells us (Rom. 8:24-25) we are saved in hope; that is, our salvation is not yet manifest. "Hope that is seen is not hope," he says, "for who hopeth for that which he seeth? But if we hope for that which we see not, then do we with patience wait for it." And Christ (Luke 12:35-36) commands,

> "Let your loins be girded about, and your lamps burning; and be ye yourselves like unto men looking for their lord, when he shall return from the marriage feast; that, when he cometh and knocketh, they may straightway open unto him."

Paul also said in the preceding epistle lesson (Titus 2:12-13),

> "We should live soberly and righteously and godly in this present world; looking for the blessed hope and appearing of the glory of the great God and our Saviour Jesus Christ."

These and similar passages prove we are even now saved and that a Christian should not seek works as a means of salvation. The delusive doctrine of works blinds the Christian's eyes, perverts a right understanding of faith and forces him from the way of truth and salvation. Salvation by grace is implied in the words, "According to his mercy he saved us," and again in the latter part of the lesson where it reads, "that we might be made heirs according to the hope of eternal life." We are heirs—though the fact is unrevealed in faith—and wait in hope for the manifestation of our inheritance.

The life of waiting we must live after we are baptized is designed to subdue the flesh and to display the power of grace in the conflict against the flesh, the world and the devil; and thus ultimately to enable us to serve our neighbors, by our preaching and example bringing them also into the faith. Though God might convert men through angels, he desires to accomplish it by human beings—by us, so that faith might be established and completed in a more congenial way through a kindred agency. Were angels constantly to dwell with us, faith would cease here. The instrumentality of angels would not be so congenial as that of our fellow-creatures, whom we are familiar with and understand. If we all were taken to heaven immediately after baptism, who would convert the others and bring them to God by means of the Word and a good example?

The fact that we expend so much by reason of purgatory and, forgetful of faith, presume to secure ourselves against purgatory or to liberate us from it by good works, unquestionably indicates we are under the influence of the devil and of Antichrist. We proceed as if our salvation were not already secured but we must gain it in some other way than by faith; and this even though plainly in contradiction of the Scriptures and of the principles of Christianity. He who does not receive salvation purely through grace, independently of all good works, certainly will never secure it. And he who makes his good works serve his own advantage, seeking to profit himself and not his neighbor thereby, performs no good work. All his doctrine is without faith and is such harmful error and deceit that I wish purgatory had never been instituted or introduced into the pulpit, for it is very destructive of Christian truth and true faith.

So great has been the devil's influence, nearly all institutions, cloister ceremonials, masses and prayers have reference simply to purgatory, leading us to the pernicious inference that through works we must improve our condition and secure salvation. So the blessings of baptism and faith must be obscured, and Christians must ultimately become pure heathen.

O Lord God, what abominable wickedness! When we should, like Christ and Paul, teach Christians to consider themselves, after baptism or absolution, ready for death at any hour and waiting for the manifestation of the salvation already theirs, we by relying on purgatory afford them indolence-fostering security. In such security they consider only this life, deferring and procrastinating in the matter of salvation until they come to their death-beds, there to effect sorrow and repentance and to presume, by ceremonials, soul-masses and bequests, to liberate themselves from purgatory. They will surely become conscious of their mistake. Now follows:

"Through the washing of regeneration, and renewing of the Holy Spirit."

How beautifully the apostle in these strong words extols the grace of God bestowed in baptism! He refers to baptism as a washing, whereby not our feet only, not our hands, but our whole bodies are cleansed. Baptism perfectly and instantaneously cleanses and saves. For the vital part of salvation and its inheritance, nothing more is necessary than this faith in the grace of God. Truly, then, are we saved by grace alone, without works or other merit. So, eternally pure love, praise and gratitude for, and honor unto, divine mercy shall possess us; we will not boast of nor delight in our own powers or achievements: as has already frequently and sufficiently been declared.

The righteousness of man, however, is a different sort of cleansing, simply a washing of garments and vessels, as recorded of hypocrites in Matthew 23:25. Externally they appear clean, but internally remain full indeed of filth. Paul terms baptism not a bodily cleansing, but a "washing of regeneration." It is not a superficial washing of the skin, a physical cleansing; it converts the whole nature, destroying the first birth, that of the flesh, with all inherited sin and condemnation.

This verse clearly indicates that salvation is not to be secured by works, but is an instantaneous gift. In physical birth we are given, not one member alone—hands or feet—but the entire body and the life; our life operates, not to effect birth, but because we are born. Similarly works do not render us pure and godly or save us: we are first made clean and godly, and receive salvation; then we freely perform good works to the honor of God and the benefit of our neighbor.

This, mark you, is the true knowledge of the pure grace of God. Thus we learn to know God and ourselves, to praise him and reject ourselves, to seek consolation from him and despair of ourselves. This doctrine is an occasion of much stumbling to them who presume to compel men to seek salvation by laws, commands and works.

For the sake of conveying a clearer understanding of this washing and this regeneration, Paul adds the word "renewing," because the individual is a new man, with a new nature. He is a new creature, with an altogether different disposition. He loves in a different way, and speaks, acts and lives in a manner unlike his former self. The apostle says (Gal.

6:15), "For neither is circumcision anything, nor uncircumcision"—that is, no work of the Law has significance—"but a new creature." The thought is: It will not do to patch up, or mend, the life here and there with works. An entirely new disposition is necessary; the nature must be changed. Then works will follow spontaneously.

Concerning this birth, Christ also declares (John 3:3), "Except one be born anew, he cannot see the kingdom of God." Here we are taught that works will not answer; the individual must himself die and obtain a different nature. This takes place in baptism when he believes, for faith is this renewing. The damned will also be born again in the last day, but theirs will be a birth without a renewing. They will remain unclean, as here in the old Adamic life. So, then, this washing, this regeneration, makes new creatures.

Much is said at various places in the Scriptures relative to the new birth. God refers to his Word and Gospel as the womb ("matricem" and "vulvam") of the new birth: "Hearken unto me, O house of Jacob, and all the remnant of the house of Israel, that have been borne by me from their birth, that have been carried from the womb" (Is. 46:3), or under my heart, as women speak of bearing children. Whosoever believes the Gospel, is conceived and born of God. But more on this subject at some other time.

We see how all these sayings overthrow works and presumptuous human mandates, and make clear the nature of faith, how the individual instantaneously and fully receives grace and is saved, works not aiding him in the matter but following as a result. Salvation by grace would be perfectly illustrated were God to produce from a dry log a live, green tree, the tree then to bring forth natural fruit. God's grace is powerful and effective. It does not, as visionary preachers presume to teach, lie dormant in the soul; nor is it an accessory to works, as the paint is an accessory to the wood. No, not so; it carries, it leads, drives, draws, changes. It effects all in man, making itself felt. Though concealed, its works are manifest. Words and works show where it is present, as the leaves and the fruit indicate the nature of the tree.

To make faith no more than an aid or ornament to works, as the sophists Thomas and Scotus, and the people, erroneously and perversely do, is a doctrine wherein faith falls far short of its real significance. For it not only aids in the accomplishment of works, but effects them unaided. Indeed, more than that, it changes and renews the whole being. Its object is to alter the character of the individual rather than to accomplish works by him. It claims to be a washing, a regeneration, a renewing, not only of works, but of the whole man.

Note, Paul here freely and fully preaches the grace of God. He does not say God has saved us by works. He loudly proclaims that God has saved us by a regeneration and a renewing. To patch up with works is unavailing; conversion of our whole nature is necessary. Therefore, believers must suffer and die before grace can manifest itself and reveal its nature. Observe, David says in this connection: "The works of Jehovah are great, sought out of all them that have pleasure therein" (Ps. 111:2). Who are these, his works? We are, sought out through grace in baptism. We are great works, new works, new born. It is indeed great that man is instantly saved, forever liberated from sin, death and hell. Hence, David says, "They are sought out of all them that have pleasure therein" or desire what God designs to accomplish through them, and God does all that man desires. But what can man desire more than to be saved, to be delivered from sin, death and hell?

Finally, the apostle terms this *washing* a "regeneration," a "renewing of the Holy Spirit," to fully express the power and efficacy of grace. This washing is a thing so vitally important it must be effected, not by a creature, but by the Holy Spirit. How completely, O holy Paul, thou dost reject the free will, the good works and the great merits of presumptuous saints! How high thou exaltest our salvation, at the same time bringing it so near to us! yes, even within ourselves. How plainly and purely thou dost preach grace. Let works, then, be here or there, to renew the man, to change the life, is impossible except by the washing of regeneration of the Holy Spirit.

That fact is plainly evident in the self-righteous. None are more intolerant, presumptuous, proud and faithless than they. In their old

Adamic nature, which they clothe and adorn with good works, they remain intractable, unrenewed and obdurate, hardened and immovable; their evil nature is unchanged. They possess only outward works. Oh, they are a people of pernicious influence, and in the sight of God wholly destitute of grace, though they imagine themselves his nearest friends.

Paul's teaching here accords with that of Christ in John 3:5, where he says, referring to the washing of regeneration: "Except one be born of water and the Spirit, he cannot enter into the kingdom of God." Note here, the water answers to the washing; to be born again, to regeneration and renewing; and the Spirit, to him whom Paul mentions as the Holy Spirit.

Note here also the apostle's apparent ignorance of the sacrament of confirmation. He teaches, as does Christ, the giving of the Holy Spirit in baptism; in baptism we are indeed born of the Holy Spirit. True, we read (Acts 8:17) how the apostles laid their hands upon those who had been baptized, that they might receive the Holy Spirit. This incident has been construed to sanction confirmation, but its real purpose was to invoke the Holy Spirit as external evidence, and the gift of divers tongues for the preaching of the Gospel. But in course of time the ceremony was abandoned. It no longer exists except in ordination or consecration to the ministerial or preaching office. Even there it is deplorably abused. But more of this at some other time.

"Which he poured out upon us richly, through Jesus Christ our Saviour."

Observe, the Holy Spirit is not merely given, but "poured out"; not only that, but "abundantly poured out." The apostle seems unable to sufficiently magnify grace and its works, while we, alas, estimate it so low in comparison to our works. It would be absurd for God to pour out upon us the Holy Spirit in such measure and yet to expect from us, and in us, something whereby we might be justified and saved; as if the superabundant divine works were insufficient.

Were such the case, Paul here must have spoken inconsiderately and might justly be accused of falsehood. But so bountifully does he represent to us the measure of grace, clearly no one can rely too much upon the washing of regeneration; it is of unlimited importance. No one can place too much confidence in it; there is always occasion for more. For God has embraced, in the Word and in faith, blessings too great for mortal life to comprehend or to receive were they to manifest themselves. As revelation begins, the individual dies; he passes out of this life, swallowed up in the blessings he now by faith apprehends in very limited measure. Thus more than abundantly are we justified and saved without works if we only believe.

Peter says, "Through Christ he hath granted unto us his precious and exceeding great promises; that through these ye may become partakers of the divine nature" (2 Pet. 1:4). He does not say "will be granted" but "hath granted." And Christ says, "For God so loved the world, that he gave his only begotten Son, that whosoever believeth on him should not perish, but have eternal life" (John 3:16). Notice, all who believe have eternal life. That being true, believers certainly are just and holy without works. Works contribute nothing to justification. It is effected by pure grace richly poured out upon us.

"But," you say, "how is it, then, the Scriptures so frequently speak of salvation for them who do good? For instance, Christ says (John 5:29), 'And shall come forth; they that have done good, unto the resurrection of life; and they that have done evil, unto the resurrection of judgment.' And Paul declares (Rom. 2:7-8) that honor and glory are the reward of them who do good; indignation and wrath, of evil-doers. And he makes many similar declarations." I answer: How are these passages to be interpreted? Not otherwise than as they read—without additions: He who does good shall be saved; he who does evil shall be damned. The difficulty lies in our error in judging according to external appearances in the matter of good works. The Scriptures teach not that way, but that no one can do good until he is himself good. He does not become good through works, but his works are good because he is good. He becomes good through the washing of regeneration and in no other way. This is the meaning of Christ's words (Matt. 7:17), "Every good tree bringeth forth good fruit; but the corrupt tree bringeth forth evil fruit." And (Matt. 12:33), "Either make the tree good, and its fruit good; or make the tree corrupt, and its fruit corrupt."

True, the self-righteous perform works similar to those of the regenerated; indeed, their works are frequently the more brilliant. They pray, fast, contribute money, erect institutions, make pilgrimages and conduct themselves with great ostentation. But Christ calls their works "sheep's clothing" (Matt. 7:15) wherein move ravening wolves. None of the self-righteous are really humble, mild, moderate and good in their hearts. This fact is revealed when one crosses them and rejects their works. Then they bring forth their natural and identifying fruits: temerity, impatience, arbitrariness, obstinacy, slander and many other evil propensities.

Therefore it is true that he who does good shall be saved—his salvation shall be revealed; but he' could do nothing good were he not already saved in the new birth. The Scriptures sometimes have reference to the external conduct of the good, and at others to their inner nature that prompts the outward works, teaching present salvation because of the inner nature, and a future salvation if good is done; that is, if the individual remains steadfast, his salvation shall be revealed in the future.

The works we performed in our old, unregenerate state, our Adamic nature, the apostle in this lesson rejects when he says "not by works done in righteousness, which we did ourselves." These may be good works, but not before God, who looks first for personal goodness and afterward for the works. In Genesis 4:4-5, he had respect first unto Abel, and then unto his offering; and first rejected Cain, and then his offering. Cain's offering, however, was in external appearance good like that of Abel.

Paul significantly adds "through Jesus Christ our Savour." The intent is to shelter us all under Christ, as young chickens are gathered under the wings of the hen. Christ himself says (Matt. 23:37), "O Jerusalem . . . how often would I have gathered thy children together, even as a hen gathereth her chickens under her wings, and ye would not!"

In the phrase above is taught the nature of true, living faith. Such is the character of faith that it is not sufficient to salvation for you to believe in God after the manner of the Jews and many others, upon whom, however, he conferred many blessings and temporal advantages; but it is through Jesus Christ you must believe in God. In the first place, you must not doubt that he is your gracious God and Father, that he has forgiven all your sins and has saved you in baptism. In the second place, you must know, too, that all this has not been effected without cause—without satisfaction having been rendered to his righteousness. There is no reason for mercy and grace to operate upon and in us, to aid us to obtain eternal blessings and salvation. Justice must first be satisfied to the fullest extent. Christ says (Matt. 5:18), "One jot or one tittle shall in no wise pass away from the law till all things be accomplished."

Whatever is promised of the grace and goodness of God must be understood as only for those who perfectly fulfil his commands. He says (Mic. 2:7) in reply to the Jews, when they presumed they were great in the sight of God and continually cried, "Peace, peace!" and, "Why should God be so angry? Why should his benign Spirit have departed from us?"—he replies, "Do not my words do good to him that walketh uprightly?" No one, therefore, can attain God's abundant grace unless he shall have rendered full satisfaction to God's commands.

Now, enough has been said to show our works of no value in God's sight, and ourselves unable to fulfil the least of his commands, to perform a single work. How much more impossible is it, then, for us to render full satisfaction to his justice and become worthy of his grace! Even though we were able to keep all his commandments and to make full satisfaction to his justice, yet we would not for that reason be worthy of his grace and of salvation. He would not be under any obligation to confer them upon us. He might require it all as obligatory upon his creatures, who must serve him. Whatever he grants is of pure grace and mercy.

This Christ clearly taught in the parable in Luke 17:7-10,

> "But who is there of you, having a servant plowing or keeping sheep, that will say unto him, when he is come in from the field, come

straightway and sit down to meat; and will not rather say unto him, Make ready wherewith I may sup, and gird thyself, and serve me, till I have eaten and drunken; and afterward thou shalt eat and drink? Doth he thank the servant because he did the things that were commanded? Even so ye also, when ye shall have done all the things that are commanded you, say, We are unprofitable servants; we have done that which it was our duty to do."

Now, if through grace and not of necessity heaven is given to those who do all they are under obligation to do; if to such—provided, such there be—heaven is given not by merit but through divine and gracious promises like that of Matthew 19:17, "If thou wouldest enter into life, keep the commandments": shall we then presume upon our wretched good works? Why extol them as if their nature and not the pure promise, the gracious Word of God, makes them worthy of the kingdom of heaven?

In the first place, God has given, a Being to fully satisfy divine justice for us all. In the second place, he has, through this same Being, poured out his grace and his rich blessings. So, then, notwithstanding grace is received by us without price and without merit on our part—indeed, in spite of great demerit and unworthiness—yet it is not bestowed without cause and deserved merit somewhere. As Paul teaches (Rom. 5:18), we fell into sin not of our own act or deserving, it being born in us from Adam in our natural birth; and on the other hand, in the new birth we enter into grace and salvation through Christ, without our merit or works.

Hence the apostle is careful in every place where he mentions grace and faith to add "through Jesus Christ," that no one may be able to say, "I believe in God and am satisfied with that." No, beloved friend, your belief must include a knowledge of how and through whom you believe. You must know that God requires you to fulfil all his commandments, to satisfy his justice, before he accepts your faith unto salvation; and that though you were able to render full satisfaction you would still have to await salvation through grace alone, and not receive it on account of any duties you perform, but rather your pride and presumption must fall to the ground before God.

Observe the advantages you have in Christ. Through him grace and salvation are conferred upon you, he having rendered full obedience to all the commandments of God, and satisfied God's justice, in your stead and for you. Grace and salvation are conferred upon you because he is worthy. This is true Christian faith.

No faith is sufficient but the Christian faith, the faith that believes in Christ and accepts solely through him the two principles—satisfaction of divine justice, and the gracious bestowal of eternal salvation. Paul, speaking of Christ (Rom. 4:25), says, "Who was delivered up for our trespasses, and was raised for our justification." Not only was he given to put away sin and to fulfil the commandments of God, but also to render us worthy, through him, of possessing righteousness and of being children of grace.

Again, Paul says of Christ (Rom. 3:25), "Whom God set forth to be a propitiation, through faith in his blood." It is not just "faith" but "faith in his blood." With his blood, and in our nature, he has rendered full satisfaction and become for us a throne of grace. We receive absolution and grace at no cost or labor on our part, but not without cost and labor on the part of Christ.

We must, then, shelter ourselves under his wings (Matt. 23:37) and not fly afar in the security of our own faith, else we will soon be devoured by the hawk. Our salvation must exist, not in our righteousness, but, as I have often said, in Christ's righteousness, which is an outspread wing, or a tabernacle, to shelter us.

Our faith and all we may have received from God is insufficient to salvation, wholly inadequate, unless faith rests beneath the wings of Christ and firmly trusts that not we but he can render, and has rendered, full satisfaction to the justice of God for us; and that grace and salvation are not conferred upon us because of our faith but because of the will of Christ. The pure grace of God, promised, procured and bestowed upon us in Christ and through Christ, must be perfectly recognized.

This is the teaching implied in John 14:6, "No one cometh unto the Father but by me." Christ's sole effort in the whole Gospel is to draw us out of ourselves into himself; he spreads out his wings and calls us together beneath their shelter. To emphasize the grace of Christ is also Paul's design in the conclusion of this lesson, where he says:

"That, being justified by his grace, we might be made heirs according to the hope of eternal life. This is a faithful saying."

He does not say "justified by our faith" but "justified by the grace of Christ." Christ alone has favor with God. No one but he has done the will of God and merited eternal life. In view of the fact that he did it not for his own sake but for ours, all believers should be so perfectly one with Christ that all he has done for them will, through him and his grace, be regarded as if the believer himself had accomplished it. See what an inexpressibly beneficent thing Christian faith is—what inconceivably great blessings it brings to all believers!

Let us learn from this epistle how precious is the Gospel that proclaims these benefits, and what injury and destruction of souls they effect who silently ignore the Gospel and preach the works of the Law, yes, their own human doctrines. Guard, then, against false preachers and also against false faith. Rely not upon yourself, nor upon your faith. Flee to Christ; keep under his wings; remain under his shelter. Let his righteousness and grace, not yours, be your refuge. You are to be made an heir of eternal life, not by the grace you have yourself received, but, as Paul says here, by Christ's grace.

Again, it is said in Psalm 91:4, "He will cover thee with his pinions, and under his wings shalt thou take refuge." And in the Song of Solomon 2:14, "O my dove, that art in the clefts of the rock, in the covert of the steep place." That is, in the wounds of Christ the soul is preserved. Observe, true Christian faith does not take refuge in itself, as the sophists dream, but flees to Christ and is preserved under him and in him.

It has been sufficiently stated that we are heirs of eternal life in hope, and that grace, regardless of works, instantaneously confers salvation, inheritance and all; yet, as said, "in hope." They are not revealed until death. Then we shall see what, in faith, we have received and possess.

THE ARMOR OF THIS EPISTLE

THIS EPISTLE LESSON forcibly and in express terms contends against all humanly-devised righteousness, as well as against all human powers and free will. These are plain words, "Not by works done in righteousness, which we did ourselves, but according to his mercy he saved us." In fact, the words of the whole lesson oppose the righteousness of man. Paul attributes all efficacy to the washing of regeneration, to the renewing of the Holy Spirit, to Jesus Christ and his grace. In the face of such thunderbolts, how can there remain in us the least trace of presumption?

It matters not how brilliant may be secular and ecclesiastical laws; how attractive the station of priests, monks and nuns; how dazzling the titles of gentlemen of honor and ladies of uprightness, even if the wearers of them could raise the dead: without faith in Christ all is vain. Such hypocrisy as that just mentioned blinds and misleads the whole world, and obscures for us the holy Gospel and the Christian faith.

These brilliant works and attractive stations of men assist as little in procuring our salvation as do the works of beasts or the common trades of mankind. Indeed, they perniciously obstruct salvation. Therefore, you should guard against wolves in sheep's clothing, and learn to cleave to Christ in true and firm faith.

7

Third Christmas Sermon

(Christmas Morning Service)

"God, having of old time spoken unto the fathers in the prophets by divers portions (at sundry times) and in divers manners, hath at the end of these days spoken unto us in his Son, whom he appointed heir of all things, through whom also he made the worlds; who being the effulgence of his glory, and the very image of his substance, and upholding all things by the word of his  power, when he had made purification of sins, sat down on the right hand of the Majesty on high; having become by so much better than the angels, as he hath inherited a more excellent name than they. For unto which of the angels said he at any time, Thou art my Son, This day have I begotten thee? And again, I will be to him a Father, And he shall be to me a Son? And when he again bringeth in the firstborn into the world he saith, And let all the angels of God worship him. And of the angels he saith, Who maketh his angels winds, And his ministers a flame of fire: but of the Son he saith, Thy throne, O God, is for ever and ever; And the sceptre of uprightness is the sceptre of thy kingdom. Thou hast loved righteousness, and hated iniquity; Therefore God, thy God, hath anointed thee With the oil of gladness above thy fellows. And, Thou, Lord, in the beginning didst lay the foundation of the earth, And the heavens are the works of thy hands: They shall perish; but thou continuest: And they all shall wax old as doth a garment; And as a mantle shalt thou roll them up, As a garment, and they shall be changed: But thou art the same, And thy years shall not fail" (Hebrews 1:1-12).

THE DIVINITY OF CHRIST

THIS IS A STRONG, forcible, noble epistle, preeminently and emphatically teaching the great article of faith concerning the Godhead, or the divinity of Christ. The presumption that it was not written by Paul is somewhat plausible, because the style is unusually ornamental for him. Some are of the opinion it was written by Luke; others by Apollos, whom Luke represents as "mighty in the

Scriptures," opposing the Jews (Acts 18:24, 28). Certain it is, no epistle enforces the Scriptures with greater power than does this. Hence it is evident the author was an eminent apostolic individual, whoever he was. Now, the object of the epistle is to establish and promote faith in the divinity of Christ, and, as already stated, scarce any portion of the Bible more strongly enforces this article of our creed. We must, therefore, confine ourselves to its words and treat it in regular order, item by item.

In the first place, it was the apostle's design to bring the Jews to the Christian faith. As we shall learn, he presses them so closely they cannot deny that Christ is true God. Now, if he is God and the Son of God, and if he himself has spoken unto us and suffered for us, justice necessarily demands our faith. We have much more reason to believe in him than had the fathers who in time past believed when God spoke simply through the prophets.

Paul contrasts the ancient preachers and disciples with those of later times. The prophets and Christ are the preachers, the fathers and ourselves the disciples. The Son, the Lord himself, speaks unto us; his servants the prophets spoke unto the fathers. If the fathers believed the servants, how much more readily would they have believed the Lord himself! And if we believe not the Lord, how much more reluctant would we have been to believe the servants! Thus he makes one condition argue for the other: our unbelief contrasted with the faith of the fathers is an awful disgrace; again, the faith of the fathers in contrast with our unbelief is deserving of very great honor.

Our disgrace is yet greater when we recall the fact that God spoke to the fathers, not only once, but at different times, and not only in one way, but in different ways; and yet they always believed; while we are not induced by their example to believe, even in one instance, the message of the Lord himself. Observe, Paul proceeds with a powerful discourse in the effort to convert the Jews, yet the attempt avails nothing.

"By divers portions (at sundry times) and in divers manners."

To me the particular and unlike meaning of these two phrases is this: "By divers portions" implies the succession of many prophets, and that all prophecies were not made through one man nor at one time; "in divers manners" signifies that through each individual prophet, to say nothing of the many, God spoke in different ways at different times. For instance, at times he expressed himself in plain, definite terms; and at other times figuratively or through visions. Ezekiel portrayed the four evangelists by the four beasts. Isaiah sometimes clearly states that Christ shall be a king; at other times he alludes to him as a rod and a branch from the stem of Jesse; again, as excellent fruit of the earth.

Thus the prophets speak of Christ in "divers manners." This latter phrase, moreover, may also be understood as implying that God spoke in various ways when he gave the people of Israel temporal aid. His leading them out of Egypt by Moses was one way of speaking, and his bringing them through the Red Sea another. In his directions to David concerning warfare and other matters he spoke in a still different way. Not one declaration, but divers declarations, were made. The objects accomplished differed. But faith was always the same—at all times and with every method.

How beautifully and gently the apostle invites and persuades the Jews when he reminds them of the fathers and the prophets, and of God himself! They had unbounded confidence in the record of these as they were in time past. But now they will not believe in God. They will not take to heart the fact of his speaking to the fathers, not once only, but often; not in one way, but in different ways. Yet they know well, and must confess that such was the case. They will not believe him now when he speaks at another time and in another way—a way he never before employed nor will again. The manner of speaking they ardently desire, will never be granted. God has never yet, not even in former time, spoken in a manner designated by them. That would be but to obstruct faith and frustrate God's design. We must leave to him the time, person and manner of speaking, and be concerned only about faith.

The phrase "at the end of these days" is significant. From now to the end no other manner of preaching is to be adopted. This is the last time he purposes to speak, and the last method he will employ. He has commanded—left on record—that this Word, and only this, is to be preached until the end. Paul says (1 Cor. 11:26), "For as often as ye eat this bread, and drink the cup, ye proclaim the Lord's death till he come." He also arrests their expectation when he says "in these days;" they are not to look for other days to come. The days when he speaks for the last time and in the last manner are already at hand.

"In his Son."

Here Paul begins to extol Christ, the last teacher, speaker and apostle: with forcible and well-grounded Scriptural evidence he shows Christ as the real Son of God and Lord over all. We must first learn to truly understand the character of Christ, that he exists in a twofold nature—divine and human. This is a point where many err. Sometimes it is to manufacture fables from his words. Men apply to the divine nature the sayings really uttered with reference to his humanity; thus are they deluded by certain passages of Scripture. It is of the utmost importance first to determine which of the statements concerning Christ pertain to his divine nature and which to his human side. This settled, all else will be easily plain.

But first we must answer the inquiry liable to be made, "If the voice of God today is the last message, why is it said that Elijah and Enoch shall come, opposing Antichrist?" I answer: Concerning the advent of Elijah, I hold that he will not come in a physical manner. (As to the coming of Elijah I am suspended between heaven and earth, but I am inclined to believe it will not take place bodily. However, I will not contend hard against the other view. Each may believe or not believe it, as he likes.) I well know St. Augustine has somewhere said, "The advent of Elijah and of Antichrist is firmly fixed in the belief of all Christians." But I also know there is no statement of Scripture to substantiate his assertion. Malachi's prophecy concerning the coming of Elijah (Mal. 4:5) the angel Gabriel makes refer to John the Baptist (Luke 1:17), and Christ does the same even more explicitly where he says (Mark 9:13), "But I say unto you, that Elijah is come, and they have also done unto him whatsoever they would, even as it is written of him." Now, if John is the Elijah of the prophecy, as the Lord here says he was, the prediction of Malachi is already fulfilled. And there is nothing more prophesied concerning the coming of Elijah. The statement the Lord made just previously to the one quoted, "Elijah indeed cometh first, and restoreth all things," may be fairly interpreted to mean that Christ, referring to the office of John, practically says, "Yes, I well know Elijah must first come and restore all things, but he has already come and accomplished it."

This view is demanded by the fact that immediately after his reference to the coming and office of Elijah, Christ speaks of his own sufferings: "It is written of the Son of man, that he must suffer many things, and be set at naught." If this prophecy concerning Christ was to be fulfilled after the coming of Elijah, then certainly Elijah must have already come. I know of nothing more to expect concerning the coming of Elijah unless it might be that his spirit will be manifest again in the power of the Word of God, as now seems probable. For I have no longer any doubt that the Pope, with the Turks, is Antichrist, whatever you may believe.

To return to Christ: We assert it is essential firmly to believe Christ true God and true man; and that the Scriptures—including Christ's own words—sometimes have reference to the divine nature of Christ and at other times to his human nature. For instance, the declaration (John 8:58), "Before Abraham was born, I am," relates to his divinity; but the statement (Matt. 20:23), "To sit on my right hand, and on my left hand, is not mine to give," recognizes his humanity, which could not help itself even on the cross. Yet some expounders have desired here to show their great skill by abstruse interpretations made to oppose the heretics. It is his human nature that says: "The Father is greater than I" (John 14:28. Also, "How often would I have gathered thy children together, even as a hen gathereth her chickens under her wings" (Matt. 23:37). Again, the passage (Mark 13:32) reading, "Of that day or that hour knoweth no one, not even the angels in heaven, neither the Son, but the Father," has reference to the man Christ.

The explanation which some have made, "The Son knew not; that is, he did not choose to reveal," is superfluous. What is the advantage of that addition? The humanity of Christ, like that of any other holy mortal man, did not, at every moment, consider and utter, did not desire and note, how some made him a man with almighty power; they improperly combine the two natures and their operation. As he did not always see, hear and feel all things, so likewise he did not at every moment contemplate in his heart every matter; he recognized things as God moved him to do, as he brought them before him. Being filled with grace and wisdom, he was able to judge and to teach as occasion demanded; the Godhead, who alone sees and knows all things, was personally present in him. Finally: All reference in the Scriptures to the humiliation and exaltation of Christ must be understood of the man; for the divine nature can neither be humiliated nor exalted.

"Whom he appointed heir of all things."

These words refer to Christ's human nature. We must believe in his supremacy in that respect as well as in his divinity. All creatures are subservient to the man Christ. As God, he creates all. As man, he creates nothing, yet all creation is subject to him. David says (Ps. 8:6), "Thou hast put all things under his feet."

Christ is our Lord and our God. As God, he creates us; as Lord, we serve him and he rules over us. The apostle refers to him in this epistle as true God, and also Lord over all. Though having two different natures, he is one person. What Christ does and suffers, essentially God does and suffers. In this case only one nature is involved.

To illustrate: I speak of a "wounded man" when but a single limb is injured. The soul is not wounded, nor is the body as a whole; only a part of the body. But I speak as I do because body and soul constitute one person. Now, as I must recognize a difference between body and soul when I speak, so must I recognize the two natures of Christ. Again: It is not a misstatement if in the night I say I have no knowledge of the sun, when at the same time I have a thorough mental knowledge of it; for I have no physical vision. Similarly, Christ knows nothing concerning the last day, and at the same time has full knowledge of it.

"Through whom also he made the worlds."

Observe, by this same Son who in his human nature is "appointed heir of all things"—by him as God, the worlds were made. He is but one person, yet with two natures of unlike operation. There is one Christ, of two natures. The terms Paul here employs are in recognition of Christ's highest nature.

Now, the apostle plainly speaks of the Son who is appointed heir when he says that by him the world is made. If everything is made by him, he could not himself have been created. Consequently, it is plain that he is true God. For anything not created and yet existing must be God. Again, whatsoever is made must be a creature and cannot be God; for it does not exist of itself but derives its existence from its Creator. Now, all things are made by Christ, and he is not created. Hence he must have his existence from himself; not from any creature nor any creator.

Furthermore, if he is a Son he is not alone, his existence necessitates a Father. Through the Son God made the world, but God cannot himself be that Son. Consequently there must be two distinct persons, the Father and the Son, yet (because) the divine nature is only one; for there cannot be more than one God. Conclusively, then, Christ with the Father is true God. In one divine substance with him, he is Creator and Maker of the world. The only difference is, one is the Son and the other the Father. And Christ is not created by the Father, as the world was created; essentially he was begotten in eternity. Nor is he inferior to the Father. He is the same in every respect except that he is begotten of the Father, and the Father not begotten of him.

If these things are beyond the grasp of our reason, reason must surrender as a captive to these and like Scripture words, and believe.

Could we comprehend this mystery by human reason, there would be no faith. Clearly enough, the words, "Through whom also he made the worlds," make mentions of two Beings. And it is not less clear that the uncreated one through whom all things were made, also must be God. Just how this can be, the Scriptures do not teach. It must be received by faith.

The Scriptures speak after this fashion: "The world is created through Christ, by the Father, in the Holy Spirit"; and though the meaning is not wholly clear, and easy of comprehension, there is good reason for the language. It is employed more by way of intimation than explanation—to imply that the Father derives not his substance from the Son, but the Son from the Father; and that the latter is the first original person in the Godhead. In the statement that the Father made the world through Christ, not Christ through the Father, the intent is to teach the Father's title to the first person; he from whom, through Christ, all things have existence. John speaks in the same way (John 1:3), "All things were made through him." And Paul again (Col. 1:16), "All things have been created through him, and unto him;" and (Rom. 11:36), "For of him, and through him, and unto him, are all things."

Note the aptness of the language where Christ is termed an "heir," in reference to his humanity. For who should be more entitled to inherit the estate of God than his Son? He with the Father created it—created all creatures. But Christ is man and Son, and because of his Sonship he inherits; in both natures is he Son. But as to the origin of the apostle's particular language, we shall learn that in the Gospel.

"Who being the effulgence (brightness) of his glory and the very image of his substance [person]."

Paul uses these figures to express with all possible clearness the fact that Christ is a person distinct from the Father, yet one, real, true God. But the German and Latin words are not just equivalent to the Greek terms employed by the apostle. The apostle speaks of Christ as the effulgence proceeding from the glory of the Father. Just as the illumination of the morning sun, the sun's vital substance, is not a part of the effulgence, but the whole effulgence of the whole sun, proceeding from the sun and yet inherent in it. By the figure, "the effulgence of his glory," is conveyed as in a word the birth of the Son, the unity of his nature and the Father's, and the distinction of the persons. Christ, without limit of time, is eternally begotten of the Father, and ever proceeds, with that unweariedness represented by the sun in the morning rather than at midday or evening. But Christ is not the person of the Father, as the effulgence is not the sun. He is with and in the Father; not existing before nor after, but co-eternal with him and a part of him, as the effulgence is with and a part of the sun.

The apostle terms the Father's effulgence "Doxa," (glory) properly implying honor or glory. Therefore the divine nature is unqualified glory and honor, having all in itself and deriving nothing from another. It has the right to boast of and glory in itself. Now, Paul says Christ is complete light, the full effulgence of God's honor. That is, he too has in himself the unlimited Godhead and has equal right with the Father to boast and glory. The only exception is, he derives his authority from the Father and not the Father from him. He is the effulgence proceeding from the paternal honor, he is God begotten and not God begetting, yet God complete and perfect as the Father is.

The Scriptures, you will observe, do not so speak of the saints, though they are also an honor to God; that is, they were created for his honor. But Paul says Christ is the brightness of the paternal honor; the words force the conclusion that the brightness constitutes the Father's honor, else it would not be the effulgence of his honor. But what shall I say by way of explanation? These words are more easily understood by the heart than explained by tongue or pen. They are in themselves clearer than any commentary renders them, and in proportion as they are explained are they obscured. The substance of the clause is this: the whole Godhead is in Christ, and to him as to God all honor is due; yet he does not derive his Godhood from himself, but from the Father. The apostle implies two persons but one God; for the Holy Spirit is not mentioned here. When we have advanced far enough to comprehend two persons existent in one God, we will readily believe in the third person.

In the other figure the apostle styles Christ an image or sign of the substance of God. Despite its clearness I still claim the privilege of speaking plainly and clearly. An image created after the likeness of a person is not an image of the substance or nature of that person. It is not a being; it is mere stone or wood. It is an image formed from stone or wood substance in the likeness of man. But if I could handle the substance of the person as the potter handles clay and make therewith an image of the individual which should also perfectly contain his substance or nature, that would, as you perceive, be an 'essential image, or a likeness of the human substance. But such would be a creature. An image necessarily is constructed from a different substance than the thing imaged, and differs in nature.

Here the Son is such an image of the Father's substance, that the Father's substance is the image itself. If we may so express it, the image is made from the Father's substance. The image is not only like the Father resembling him, but fully contains his whole substance and nature; as it may be said of "the effulgence of his glory," that the effulgence is constituted of the glory, and not only like it but embodying it perfectly, making the effulgence and the glory identical.

Now notice, as I say an image of man is formed of wood or stone, so I say Christ is a divine image: as truly as the former is but a material image, so truly is the latter God. Paul calls Christ the image of the living and invisible God.

In the wooden image, this perfection is lacking. Though a wooden image, it is not an image of the wood but of an individual; it does not represent the woods but the individual. Though the individual be faithfully reproduced in the wood, yet he himself is not wood; his substance is something different from the substance imaging him. In all cases the image differs in substance from the person imaged. It is impossible to furnish an image actually the substance of the individual. But in this verse we have an image and one imaged who are identical in substance, except that the Father is not an image. The Father is not fashioned from nor like the Son; but the Son from the Father, and is like the Father, in one simple, truly divine substance with him.

Such perfection is also wanting in the sun and its effulgence. The sun has its own splendor, and the same is true of its effulgence, but the effulgence derives its splendor from the sun. But in the figure before us, effulgence is splendor; of the splendor, if we may so speak, the effulgence is constituted. The splendor is essentially and perfectly the effulgence itself, with this difference that the effulgence has not its origin in itself but in the paternal splendor.

You will notice the verse is even now clearer than the explanation. "The image of his substance," "the effulgence of his glory"—these Paul's sayings are clear enough. The tongue should be silent here to allow the heart to reflect. The Hebrew mode of speaking is thus:

> "Pauperes sanctorum, i. pauperes sancti; Virtus Dei, i. virtus Deus; Sic, character substantiæ;, i. character substantia, subsistens et impsemet Deus; Sic, splendor gloriæ, i. splendor gloria ipsa."

Latin scholars may easily comprehend this, but for the Germans and the common people it suffices to call the likeness made from gold an image of gold. Similarly, they are to call Christ an image of God the Father because he is wholly of God in character, and there is no God beside him, though at the same time his Godhead and image have origin from the Father as the first person; but the two are one God. This is not true of creatures. The golden image represents not a golden nature, but the wholly different nature of the individual. Though it is a golden image, it does not image the nature of gold. Another image is necessary to represent the nature of gold; as, for instance, a golden color, or something else not truly gold.

But in our text the image is also the substance of the imaged, and no other image is requisite than its own substance. It is faith that is called for here and not keen speculation. The words are clear enough; they are positive and forcible. He who will not in them recognize the divinity of Christ, will not recognize it in any way. Christ is not here termed a common image in the ordinary sense of the word; the word used is "Character"—an image more characteristic than a portrait or any other likeness. Again, he is called "Apaugasma"—an actual brightness resembling nothing but the glory from which it proceeds.

"And upholding all things by the word of his power."

For a third time Christ is represented as God. First, it is stated that the worlds were made by him; second, he is called the brightness and the image of God; and here he upholds all things. If he upholds all, he is not himself upheld. He is supreme, hence he must be God. To uphold all things is to support and maintain them. Not only are all things made by him, as stated in the preceding verse, but they are perpetuated and preserved by him. As Paul says in Colossians 1:17: "In him all things consist." The word "upholding" is well chosen. Christ neither coerces nor restrains nor disturbs the peace; he gently sustains, permitting all creatures to enjoy his tender goodness. As it is written in the Wisdom of Solomon 8:1: "Wisdom reacheth from one end to another mightily; and sweetly doth she order all things."

I am not fully decided as to the intent of the phrase "by the word of his power." Were these the words of uninspired man, I would think the writer in error; for Christ is himself the Word, as the Gospel teaches, and acts in obedience to no word. Did they refer to the person of the Father, it would be perfect harmony with the Scripture teaching; for the Father made all things through his Word and upholds them in that Word. As said in Psalm 33:6, "By the word of Jehovah were the heavens made."

I withhold my view to give place to another and better one. I merely venture the opinion that the apostle's purpose in this manner of speaking may be to emphasize the unity of the persons in one Godhead. Since they are one God, we may understand here reference to the Father; God's action is the action of each of the three persons. God upholds all things by his Word; Christ, or the Word here mentioned, is really God.

There are other places in the Scriptures where we have a sudden change of person. For instance, Psalm 2:6-7: "Yet have I set my king upon my holy hill of Zion. I will tell of the decree: Jehovah said unto me, Thou art my Son." There the first verse represents the Father speaking concerning the Son: and the second verse, the Son concerning the Father. The reason for the sudden change of persons in this brief passage is, the two persons are one God. It may be that when our text declares that one is the image of God, the reference is to Christ; and that when it states one upholds all things by his word, reference is to the Father, no designation being made because the two are one God without distinction.

If this is not a satisfactory conclusion, we might regard the expression in this light: we might understand the term "word" as having somewhat the significance of an event or act. For instance, in the Gospel (Luke 2:15) we read of the shepherds saying: "Let us now go even unto Bethlehem, and see this thing (word—event) that is come to pass"—let us see the event which has taken place there. So, in this phrase declaring Christ upholds all things by the word of his power, we might understand "by the act of his power." By the operation of his power are all things preserved; and all existence and power are derived not from the things themselves but from the active power of God. Further, power and the Word are not to be divorced; they are identical. We may say of an efficient word that its nature and substance are the operating power. Now, each may adopt the view to him most plausible.

"When he had by himself made purification of our sins."

Here the apostle touches upon the Gospel proper. Whatever we may be taught concerning Christ is without significance to ourselves until we learn we are the beneficiaries of the doctrine. What would be the advantage to us of preaching were it designed alone for Christ's benefit? The fact is, these words concern only us; they have to do with our salvation. Let us, then, joyfully listen. The language is incomparably beautiful, telling that the supreme Christ, the heir of all things, the effulgence of God's glory and the image of his substance; who upholds all things, not by extraneous power, not with assistance, but by his own power, his own act; who, in short, is all in all—that he has come to serve us, has poured out his love for us and made purification for our sins.

The apostle says "our," "our sins;" not his own sin, not the sins of unbelievers. Purification is not for, and cannot profit, him who does not believe. Nor did Christ effect the cleansing by our free-will, our reason or power, our works, our contrition or repentance, these all being worthless in the sight of God; he effects it by himself. And how? By taking our sins upon himself on the holy cross, as Isaiah 53:6 tells us.

But even this answer does not sufficiently explain how he cleanses us "by himself." To go further: When we accept him, when we believe he has purified us, he dwells within us because of, and by, our faith, daily continuing to cleanse us by his own operation; and nothing apart from Christ in any way contributes to the purification of our sins. Note, he does not dwell in us, nor work our cleansing through himself, by any other way than in and through our faith.

Hearken, then, ye deceivers of the world and blind leaders of the blind; ye Pope, ye bishops, priests, monks, learned and idle talkers; who teach the purification of sins by human achievements, and that satisfaction for sins may be made by men; who issue indulgences and vend devised purifications of sins. Listen to the teaching here: Purification of sins is not effected by human effort, but solely in Christ and through himself. Christ is communicated to us, not through any work of ours, but through faith alone, as Paul teaches in Ephesians 3:17 that "Christ dwells in your hearts through faith." Plainly, then, the purification of sins is faith, and he who believes that Christ has purged his sins, unquestionably is cleansed through that faith and in no other way. Appropriate, then, is Peter's expression in Acts 15:9, "cleansing their hearts by faith."

Having once possessed faith, and purification being effected in us by Christ, we are then to perform good works, hating our sins and repenting of them. Under these conditions our works are really good. Before faith is present, they avail naught; rather they induce false confidence and trust. So heinous an evil are our sins, and so enormous is the cost of their purification, it was necessary that one exalted as we here read Christ was, must intervene to purge them by himself. What could the poor, vain attempts of us who are creatures, and besides sinful, feeble, corrupt creatures, accomplish where the demand was of such magnitude? One might as reasonably presume to burn heaven and earth with an extinguished brand. Our sins can be expiated only by a price commensurate with the God they offend.

"Sat down on the right hand of the Majesty on high; having become by so much better than the angels, as he hath inherited a more excellent name than they."

This statement refers to the human nature of Christ wherein he effected the purification of our sins; at the same time it is true the cleansing was an achievement of the Son of God. We must not, in making distinction of natures, try to make a distinction of persons. Again, we may truly say the Son of God sits on the right hand of the Majesty, though the passage is to be accepted only in the human sense, for in his divine nature he is himself the only Majesty, in unity with the Father, upon whose right hand he sits. But we will abandon these comments which but obscure, and keep to the clearer language of the text.

To "sit on the right hand of the Majesty" certainly implies a likeness to that Majesty. Wherever it is said that Christ sits at the right hand of God, there is fundamentally established his title to true God; for no one but God himself is like God. So, to say that the man Christ sits on the right hand of God is equivalent to saying he is true God. Psalm 110:1 declares, "Jehovah saith unto my Lord, Sit thou at my right hand." That is, Jehovah said to Christ the man: Be like me; in other words, Thou shalt be recognized not simply as man but as God. It is with this thought the apostle cites the psalmist.

Again, it is written (Ps. 8:6), "Thou hast put all things under his feet." That is, Thou hast made him equal with thyself. Not that Christ was not God until all things were put under his feet. But his humanity was not yet God and equal with God. For as soon as he began to be man, he began to be God. The Scriptures refer to Christ in terms more appropriately significant than we are accustomed to use. So far at times is the person lost sight of in the nature, or the natures so strongly distinguished, few rightly comprehend the words. I have myself frequently erred in passages of this character, attributing to the nature that which concerns the person, and vice versa. In Philippians 2:6-8 we read,

> "Who, existing in the form of God, counted not the being on an equality with God a thing to be grasped, but emptied himself, taking the form of a servant, being made in the likeness of men; and being found in fashion as a man."

This passage, however, is obscure.

To return to our text: Note, the apostle now begins to cite the Old Testament for Scripture testimony that Christ is God. Up to this time he has given us his own views and used his own language, based on his interpretations of Scripture. He has told us Christ is far superior to the angels for he has become God and has by inheritance obtained a more excellent name than they. His whole design is to show the man Christ, becoming God, being recognized and glorified as God.

"For unto which of the angels said he at any time, Thou art my Son, this day have I begotten thee?"

This quotation is from the second Psalm. To make plainer the apostle's allusion to Christ, we cite the entire Psalm, as follows:

> "Why do the nations rage, and the peoples meditate a vain thing? The kings of the earth set themselves, and the rulers take counsel together, against Jehovah, and against his anointed, saying, Let us break their bonds asunder, and cast away their cords from us. He that sitteth in the heavens will laugh: the Lord will have them in derision. Then will he speak unto them in his wrath, and vex them in his sore displeasure: Yet I have set my king upon my holy hill of Zion. I will tell of the decree: Jehovah said unto me, Thou art my son; this day have I begotten thee.

Ask of me, and I will give thee the nations for thine inheritance, and the uttermost parts of the earth for thy possession. Thou shalt break them with a rod of iron; thou shalt dash them in pieces like a potter's vessel. Now therefore be wise, O ye kings: be instructed, ye judges of the earth. Serve Jehovah with fear, and rejoice with trembling. Kiss the son, lest he be angry, and ye perish in the way, for his wrath will soon be kindled. Blessed are all they that take refuge in him."

We see plainly, the reference here is to Christ, against whom raged the Jews, with Pilate, Herod and the chief priests. To Christ, God says, "Thou art my Son."

The Jews endeavor to evade this passage of the apostle by introducing wild interpretations. Unable to deny that the Psalm refers to a coming king and anointed one—or Christ, as "anointed" implies—they assert the allusion is to David, who was also a Christ. For they term all kings "messiahs" or "christs"—anointed ones. But their position will not hold. David never inherited the heathen, nor did his kingdom extend to the uttermost parts of the earth, as recorded of the king mentioned in the Psalm. Again, in no instance in the Scriptures is it said to any man, "Thou art my Son."

Even when the Jews do admit the Psalm's allusion to the Messiah they resort to two evasions. They maintain he is yet to come, that Jesus Christ is not the Messiah. Further, that despite being called the Son of God, he is not God. For, they say, it is written of the children of God in general (Ps. 82:6): "I said, Ye are gods, and all of you sons of the Most High"; and many times in the Scriptures the saints are called the children of God (Gen. 6:2; Ps. 89:27; Matt. 5:45; 1 John 3:2); Paul, too, in various places calls us children of God, and we in return call him Father, as in the Lord's Prayer.

How shall we reply to them? Shall we leave the apostle unsustained, as if he had not given good, clear Scripture proof? To do so would be unjust. In the first place, we have the testimony of experience that Jesus is he of whom the Psalm speaks; in Christ the prophecy is fulfilled and become history. He was persecuted by kings and rulers. They sought to destroy him and only brought derision upon themselves in the attempt.

They were themselves destroyed, as the Psalm says. Throughout the world Christ is recognized Lord. No king, before nor since, has ruled or can rule in equal extent. Now, if in Christ the Psalm is fulfilled, it cannot be made to refer to any other.

Admitting the saints are called "gods" and "the children of God," the apostle's reasoning based on the fact that nowhere is it said to any angel, much less to any man, "Thou art my Son," sufficiently proves that Christ is God. He must be peculiarly God's Son, having a relation unshared by men and angels. The fact that God does not include him among other sons but especially distinguishes him, indicates his superiority. He cannot be superior to angels without being true God, for angels are the highest order of beings.

Further, God begets all other children through some agency. For instance, James 1:18, "Of his own will he brought us forth by the word of truth." Angels are not begotten, but are created. The Son, however, God did not create; he begat him through himself. He says: "I, I myself—by myself I have begotten thee this day." Such language is not employed with reference to any other. This personal bringing forth of a single Being embraces a natural birth. True, God says of Solomon (1 Chron. 22:10), "He shall be my son;" but he does not make to him the personal declaration, "Thou art my Son, this day have I begotten thee." David begat Solomon, but the one referred to was begotten by God alone.

Again, God says "this day;" that is, in eternity. Natural birth cannot be effected in a day, as witness the human species as well as the animals. To specify concerning this particular birth, God adds "this day." He begets his Son instantaneously—eternally; begetting and bringing forth are simultaneous. God does not say, "I begat thee a year ago;" it is now—"Thou art my Son, I have begotten thee." Essentially, then, it is a transcendental birth, a birth of an exalted nature and incomprehensible to man.

According to Hosea 11:1, God says he called his son out of Egypt. This verse, like the Psalm, implies the Son of God. The Jews assert the reference is to the people of Israel, but Matthew (2:15) applies it to

Christ. But however this may be, nowhere in the Scriptures do we find it said to any man, not even to a renowned king, "Thou art my Son." Much less do we find where God says to any man, "I myself have begotten thee—this day have I begotten." Hence it is plainly evident from the Psalm that Jesus is the Christ and the true, natural Son of God.

Mark you, so much emphasis does the apostle lay upon Scriptural authority, we are under no obligation to accept anything the Bible does not assert. Were not this true, his argument, "Unto which of the angels said he at any time," etc., would not be conclusive. The Jews might say, "Notwithstanding God did not in the Scriptures make such assertion to the angels, he may have otherwise asserted it; for the Scriptures do not record everything." Now, if in the purpose of God we are under no obligation to accept anything not presented in the Scriptures, we are also to reject all doctrines not taught therein.

This conclusion operates against the presumption of the Pope and his followers, who shamelessly assert we must accept more than the Scriptures present. They claim it is not conclusive reasoning to say of a certain thing, "It is not in the Scriptures, therefore it is not authentic." They oppose the apostle's teaching even to greater extent than do the Jews, introducing their councils, teachers and high schools. Beware of their error. Be certain you have full Scripture authority for all you accept. Of whatever is not in the Scriptures, ask as does the apostle here, "When did God ever assert it?"

"And again, I will be to him a Father, and he shall be to me a Son."

The Catholics also impair the force of this passage. Apparently the purpose of their teaching is but to weaken the point of the Scriptures. They assert the verse has two meanings: first, it refers to Solomon as a figure of Christ; second, to Christ directly. But to admit the Scriptures to be of uncertain meaning would be immediately to make them not conclusive. The Jews might maintain that reference is to Solomon primarily. Then the apostle apparently would be overthrown and would establish nothing. So we should firmly hold that Christ alone is here spoken of, even as the preceding verse presents a Son peculiar and above all other sons. If the word was not spoken to angels, much less was it to Solomon. The apostle says this Son has obtained a more excellent name than the angels; therefore, by no means can the reference be to Solomon.

We are not to be content merely to accept the apostle's statement; we are under obligation to show how he clearly and conclusively establishes his position. Know, then, he cites 2 Samuel 7:14 and Psalm 89:26. The books named are prophetic. In the passages adduced the reference is to Christ alone; not to Solomon. But in 1 Chronicles 22:10, a historical book, reference is had to Solomon alone: "He shall be my son, and I will be his father." Even the Jews admit the true Christ is alluded to in Psalm 89:26-27, "He shall cry unto me, Thou art my Father, my God, and the rock of my salvation. I also will make him my first-born, the highest of the kings of the earth." Likewise is the reference to Christ in verse 6: "Who among the sons of the mighty is like unto Jehovah [the Lord]?" The meaning is: Among the sons of God is one who is God, and no one is like unto the Lord.

Though the passages in 2 Samuel and 1 Chronicles are in harmony, yet such are the circumstances forming the setting in the first passage, the word cannot be understood to refer to Solomon. The two texts must be two different declarations to David, one concerning Christ and one concerning Solomon. In the first instance (Psalm 7:12), God says to David: "When thy days are fulfilled, and thou shalt sleep with thy fathers, I will set up thy seed after thee, that shall proceed out of thy bowels."

Now, Solomon was not set up king subsequent to David's death, but while David yet lived (1 Kgs. 1:30ff). David well knew the declaration was made concerning Christ. It is for that reason he expressed heartfelt praise to God, saying (2 Sam. 7:19), "O Lord Jehovah, thou hast spoken also of thy servant's house for a great while to come." While he himself lived, David ordained Solomon his successor. He says (1 Chron. 22:8-10), "The word of Jehovah came to me saying . . . A son shall be born to thee, who shall be a man of rest . . .

He shall build a house for my name;" not thou who "hast shed blood abundantly." In the passage from Samuel nothing is said about the shedding of blood. There God says he will build a house for David. Further argument for the idea advanced is found in the fact that in 2 Samuel 7:14-15 God freely unqualifiedly promises, "If he commit iniquity, I will chasten him with the rod of men, and with the stripes of the children of men; but my loving-kindness shall not depart from him." He freely promises his grace for the things so bitterly bewailed in Psalm 89.

As Psalm 132:12 shows, the promise made concerning Solomon is made only upon the condition, "If thy children will keep my covenant," etc. This David indicates in 1 Kings 2:4, and God makes it known to Solomon in the following chapter, verse 14. The passage from Samuel, then, should be understood particularly to refer to Christ, but not that from Chronicles. This is clearly and conclusively proven.

"And when he again bringeth in the firstborn into the world he saith, And let all the angels of God worship him."

Here we have cited a third passage from Psalm 97 (verse 7), which clearly speaks of the kingdom of God, whereof Christ in the Gospel teaches. In this kingdom Christ reigns; he is Lord. It had its beginning after his ascension and is completed through the preaching of the Gospel; for it plainly alludes to preaching. It reads:

> "Jehovah reigneth; let the earth rejoice; let the multitude of isles be glad. Clouds and darkness are round about him [that is, he reigns in faith concealed]: righteousness and justice are the foundation of his throne. A fire goeth before him, and burneth up his adversaries round about. His lightnings lightened the world [these are his miracles]: the earth saw and trembled. The mountains [the great rulers, and the proud] melted like wax at the presence of Jehovah, at the presence of the Lord of the whole earth. The heavens [the apostles] declare his righteousness [faith], and all the peoples have seen his glory [for the Gospel is everywhere preached]. Let all them be put to shame that serve graven images, that

boast themselves of idols: worship him, all ye gods. Zion heard and was glad and the daughters of Judah rejoiced, because of thy judgments."

Experience and its fulfilment explain this Psalm. It was completely fulfilled in Christ. He is preached in all the world and reigns in the kingdom of God, which is not true of any other king. The apostle prefaces his quotation with the words, "And again, when he bringeth in the first-begotten into the world," meaning that in the Psalm the Spirit speaks of the second coming of Christ into the world through the Gospel. He came first in bodily form. Through the instrumentality of his crucifiers he was driven out in death. But afterward, in his resurrection and in the Word, he re-entered the world and now reigns with authority. Nevermore will he die nor be driven out. It is of this second entrance the Psalm speaks.

The author of the epistle practically says, "I grant God has other sons, but it is the first-born son whom he brings into the World a king and whom the angels worship, which the angels would not do, nor would be commanded to do, were he not true God."

True, we read of David and many others being worshiped, but not by angels. No angel ever yet adored any but God. This passage proves that he whom angels reverence must be God. For since even men worship on earth only what is superior to themselves, and with angels only God is superior, that king whom ministers herald in the world and angels worship must be God. That the apostle does not cite the whole Psalm literally is of no significance. The language of the Psalm is: "Worship him, all ye gods," while the apostle says, "Let all the angels of God worship him." The meaning, however, is the same. The thought is of future action—the angels shall worship him. If so, he must be God. The angels are his, though he is himself man. Note, however, in the Hebrew the passage reads: "Worship him, all ye Elohim"; that is, all ye gods. The term is given to angels, and to saints in general, because they are the children of God.

"And of the angels he saith, Who maketh his angels winds [spirits], and his ministers a flame of fire."

The apostle's intent here is to show that in the Scriptures the angels are not spoken of in terms that make possible a reference to them in the statements, "Thou art my Son," "He shall be my Son," "All the angels shall worship him." They are simply appointed messengers sent forth of God into the world. Although to them he has committed much, he does not constitute any among them Lord; they are characterized as wind and a flame of fire. He terms them "spirits," "winds" and "a flame of fire" because in such form do they execute his bidding, moving with the ease and swiftness of the wind, and having the brilliance of lightning or a flame of fire, as much Scriptural evidence testifies. Yet no one of them is withal Lord of the world and heralded everywhere in the manner the king here mentioned is proclaimed Lord over all things. Even the Jews must confess that.

"But of the Son he saith, Thy throne, O God, is for ever and ever; and the sceptre of uprightness is the sceptre of thy kingdom. Thou hast loved righteousness, and hated iniquity; therefore God, thy God, hath anointed thee with the oil of gladness above thy fellows."

This fourth quotation is from Psalm 45:6-7. To me it most clearly and forcibly proves Christ to be God. Even the Jews cannot oppose that interpretation. Let us consider: In the first place, it is universally acknowledged the Psalm refers to Christ, even were we to grant he is yet to come, as the Jews erroneously presume. In the second place, the first sentence, "Thy throne, O God, is for ever and ever," necessarily relates to the true God to whom throne and government belong. Though saints are sometimes termed "gods," as we learned from Psalm 82:1, yet government and throne are the prerogative of none but the one true and actual God. Is not this indisputably plain? So, then, this God upon the throne who reigns eternally is our true God.

Then the succeeding sentence is spoken of the same God: "Thou hast loved uprightness . . . therefore God, even thy God, hath anointed thee . . . above thy fellows." What is implied? That the God upon the everlasting throne, who reigns eternally, is anointed by his God above all his fellows. He who here anoints must certainly be the true God; and also the anointed must be actual God because of his throne and eternal reign. Now, God does not anoint himself; the anointed is subordinate to the one anointing. "To anoint" here implies, to infuse the Holy Spirit, with his graces; something to be exercised only upon a creature.

Note that indisputably the first part of the passage makes the king in question true God, and the latter part true man. In his humanity he has fellows, for he is the head of all believers, and they are partakers of the Spirit he possesses abundantly and above all others. But in his divinity he has no fellows; for there is only one God—one God but not one person. The passage forces the conclusion that there are two persons, one who reigns and another who anoints and whose divinity will not admit of his being himself anointed. Hence we must conclude the King is the Son of God; his title is ascribed because he is God. His eternal throne is the kingdom introduced after Christ's ascension. Yet he has fellows, is anointed, and deservedly anointed because he loves righteousness; things wholly characteristic of actual man.

The rod or scepter of the Son's kingdom is the Gospel. It is a scepter of uprightness because aggressive for the right and taking a straight course. This declaration stands opposed to human doctrines, which abound in intricacies and perplexities and yet contribute nothing to salvation. It is another reminder that we are to accept nothing in all Christendom but the scepter of Christ's kingdom. He would have his kingdom ruled by no other scepter than that righteous one, the Gospel.

It is necessary to use the word "God" twice in the latter part of the verse—"God, thy God"—because our language has but one word for that meaning. The Hebrew tongue has many, employing here these two, "Elohim" and "Elohe."

In the Old Testament are many similar passages, mysteriously used but unquestionably conclusive upon this matter; for instance, Genesis 19:24, "Jehovah rained upon Sodom and upon Gomorrah brimstone and fire from Jehovah out of heaven." What can it mean—"Jehovah," "from Jehovah,"—but that two persons are indicated, the Father and the Son? Again (Zech. 3:2), "Jehovah said unto Satan, Jehovah rebuke thee, O Satan." Observe here, God himself speaks of another God. And again, in Psalm 68, where frequent mention is made of God, it is stated (verse 18): "Thou hast ascended on high, thou hast led away captives." With respect to ascension, however, reference is only to the man Christ. Again, in the same Psalm (verse 28) we have, "Thy God hath commanded thy strength." Further, it says God commands the power of God. And there are many similar passages.

"And, Thou, Lord, in the beginning didst lay the foundation of the earth, and the heavens are the works of thy hands; they shall perish; but thou continuest: and they all shall wax old as doth a garment; and as a mantle shalt thou roll them up, and they shall be changed: but thou art the same, and thy years shall not fail."

How this quotation testifies that Christ is God is not at once apparent. As written, it easily seems to refer to God as one person. But we must take into consideration the entire Psalm. The Psalm speaks of the future kingdom of God, direction of which the Scriptures assign to Christ. Among the various passages concerning Christ's kingdom is a portion of this last-cited Psalm (Ps. 102:12-16):

> "But thou, O Jehovah, wilt abide for ever; and thy memorial name unto all generations. Thou wilt arise, and have mercy upon Zion; for it is time to have pity upon her, yea, the set time is come. For thy servants [the apostles] take pleasure in her stones, and have pity upon her dust. [That is, through the Gospel. Reference is to Christ, whose servants the apostles are bringing the stones of Zion—the elect—to grace, through their preaching. Such servants no earthly king ever had.] So the nations shall fear the name of Jehovah, and all the kings of the earth thy glory. For Jehovah hath built up Zion; he hath appeared in his glory."

The Psalm concludes with, "And thou, Lord, in the beginning hast laid the foundation of the earth." The psalmist's evident conclusion is: The King whose servants have favored the stones of Zion, who is proclaimed worldwide and commands the fear of the heathen and all the kings of the earth, is the God who created the earth and is in himself unchangeable. No earthly king has ever been proclaimed among all the heathen as Christ has been proclaimed. Christ, then, is true God and true man. What further comment the subject demands I leave for keener minds.

So we see this whole epistle lesson is simply armor to clearly maintain the article of faith that Christ is God, and Lord over all things even in his humanity. We note with amazement the perfect clearness of the Scripture teaching and that the defect is in ourselves, unperceived. Well does Luke speak (Luke 24:32) of Christ's opening the understanding of the disciples to comprehend the Scriptures. It was not the Scriptures he opened, but their understanding; the former is plain, but our eyes are not fully open.

Printed in Dunstable, United Kingdom